ANATOMY OF THE
CASTLE

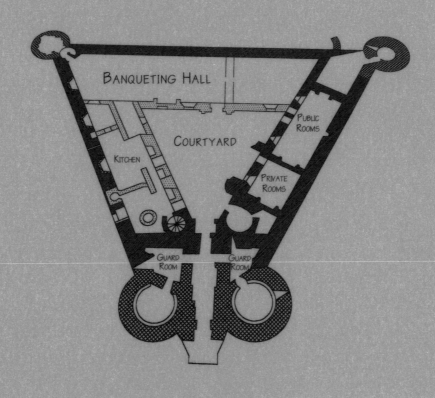

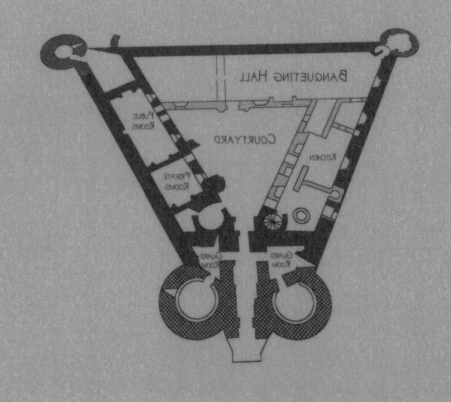

ANATOMY OF THE
CASTLE

John Gibson

MetroBooks

ACKNOWLEDGMENTS AND PHOTO CREDITS

The author would like to thank Sara Hunt for advice and encouragement during the writing of this book. The publisher gratefully acknowledges the following individuals and institutions for their assistance: Sara Hunt, editor; Robin Langley Sommer, copy editor; Simon Ethan Saunders, managing editor; Nikki L. Fesak, graphic designer; Erin Pikor, production assistant and artist; Charles J. Ziga, design direction; Clare Haworth-Maden, indexer; Glenn O. Myers, for the research and use of historical images in his collection; Lottie van Grieken; Jeanette Limondjian; Erica Heisman. Particular thanks are due to the photographers and artists whose images appear on the pages listed below:
© Colin Baxter: page 1 photograph; © Kindra Clineff: 2, 86–87, 144–45, 176–77, 192; © Kathy Collins: 17 (top), 18/23 (outside of gatefold), 19–22 (gatefold), 25, 31, 114–15, 131 (below), 138–39, 142, 143, 146–47, 148–49, 160–61, 179, 180–81, 182–83, 186/191 (outside of gatefold), 187–90 (gatefold), 196–97; © Nikki L. Fesak: 3, 26–27, 29, 34–35, 44, 46–47 (all), 49, 54–55, 64, 73, 74, 75 (below), 76–77, 78, 80–81 (all), 84–85, 90, 111, 112, 116, 118–19 (all), 122, 123, 125 (top), 126, 127 (top), 128 (below), 129 (below), 130 (top), 132 (both), 133 (top), 135, 150, 151, 152, 153, 163, 167, 168; © Jan Butchofsky Houser: 14, 117, 120–21, 157, 193; © Dave G. Houser: 11, 124, 125 (below), 136–37, 170, 198–99; © Wolfgang Kaehler: 6–7, 12, 17 (below), 24, 96, 97, 98/103 (outside of gatefold), 99, 100–02 (gatefold), 104, 106, 107, 108, 109, 141, 154, 166, 169, 171 (both), 174 (all), 175, 184, 185, 194, 195; © Christine Osborne/Middle East Pictures: 58/63 (outside of gatefold), 59, 65, 70, 70–71, 72; © P. Patel/Middle East Pictures: 60–62 (gatefold); © J. Worker/Middle East Pictures: 57; © Charles J. Ziga: 30, 33, 43, 45, 50, 51, 52–53 (all), 88, 93, 94–95 (all), 127 (below), 128 (top), 129 (top), 130 (below), 131 (top), 133 (below), 134, 158–59, 164, 165, 182. Saraband Image Library: 8, 172, 173. Artwork: © Seamus Moley: page 1 (overlay diagram); © Erin Pikor: 36, 39, 41, 48, 82 (hand coloring), 91; © James P. Rodey III: 16 (hand coloring); 28 (hand coloring), 202.

TO DAUGHTER CLARE, WHO HAS BEEN THERE, AND GRANDSON ROBERT MALAN DE MÉRINDOL, WHOSE FOREBEARS BUILT A CASTLE

MetroBooks

An Imprint of
Friedman/Fairfax Publishers

©2001 Saraband (Scotland) Limited

This edition published by Metrobooks by arrangement with Saraband

ISBN 1-58663-194-2

1 3 5 7 9 10 8 6 4 2F

For bulk purchases and special sales, please contact:
Friedman/Fairfax Publishers
Attention: Sales Department
15 West 26th Street
New York, NY 10010
212/685-6610 FAX 212/685-1307

Visit our website:
www.metrobooks.com

Page 1: An aerial view of Caerlaverock Castle, Dumfries, Scotland, with its unusual triangular ground plan.

Page 2: Tower detail at the elegant Alcàzar of Segovia, Spain.

Page 3: An unyielding portcullis at Coca Castle, Spain.

CONTENTS

THE EVOLUTION
OF
FORTIFICATIONS

Below: Château de Saumur. This well-known miniature from a fifteenth-century manuscript, Les Très Riches Heures du Duc de Berry, *has greatly contributed to our modern, idealized views of a romantic medieval era, epitomized by this graceful, gleaming castle with its many towers and turrets. This picture, known to be remarkably accurate, depicts the month of September, with the grapes being harvested in the castle's vineyard.*

"Castle": the very word conjures up vivid images in the Western mind. Castles are embedded so deeply in our consciousness, and are so entwined in our myths, legends and fairy tales, that it can be difficult to separate fact from fiction, to differentiate among the romance, the evil, the delight and the fear. Are they a symbol of suppression, dominance, treachery and great cruelty, or a reminder of the age of chivalry, courtly love, fair maidens in distress and gallant knights in shining armor saving them from fates worse than death? Do castles epitomize the deep yearning we all experience for security and a safe refuge, as demonstrated by the inclusion of their images in so many modern advertisements, or rather a desire for power and glory? Whatever the answer to these quasi-rhetorical questions, it is beyond dispute that castles are deeply rooted in our cultural heritage.

The aim of this book is to sort out fact from myth and to explain why castles existed at all, why they are situated where we see them (or their ruins!) today, how they were built and how their structure reflected the threats they were designed to counter. Fortifications have existed for as long as *Homo sapiens* had anything to defend—since people learned how to cultivate the soil and settle on it with domesticated animals. Sadly, there has never been any lack of predatory humans who were prepared to attack and seize others' land and possessions by force, and to make slaves of any survivors. The interaction between methods of defense that were developed for protection, and the means of overthrowing them, led to the evolution of increasingly sophisticated fortifications, followed by improved developments in siege warfare designed to overthrow them.

WHAT IS A CASTLE?

Although we shall consider this iterative reaction more closely later, the definition of a castle, as described in this volume, should be clarified here. A castle was the fortified residence of a lord, and reflected the militarily dominated social structures of the Middle Ages. It was essentially a product of the feudal system, and its decline in significance coincided with the end of this vital stage in the development of the systems of government we have in Europe and the Americas today. A "lord" was the person who had, and could maintain by military means, virtually absolute power over the territory surrounding his castle, either directly, in most cases, or by delegating to a subordinate or castellan.

When a lord was absent—which was often the case with sovereigns and great noblemen—his representative would act for him and administer all the dependent estates. Thus a castle was not a fort, occupied by a garrison, nor was it a fortified settlement or city, although the evolving designs and structures of all three were interdependent, as were the means of attacking them.

We shall consider the development of those fortifications that qualify as the "ancestors" of the medieval castle in Europe and the Near East. A comprehensive study of all kinds of fortification would require a sound knowledge of several disciplines, including history (political, social, economic and military), plus archaeology, geography and architecture. Limitations of space dictate that we concentrate mainly on military aspects, remembering, however, that these are merely the outcome, or reflection, of the contemporary societies that produced them.

THE EVOLUTION OF FORTIFIED SETTLEMENTS

The emergence of agriculture during the Neolithic Revolution, around 9000–8000 BC, produced a surplus of domesticated animals and crops, which enabled towns to become viable propositions. Inevitably, plundering raids by predatory nomads followed, and also fueled the desire for conquest in neighboring cities and states. Thus defensive fortifications became a necessity. Jericho, founded around 8500 BC, is thought to have been the first walled town in the world. While the intention here is not to examine the general effect all this had on developing cultures—"civilization," as it is called—it certainly brought about the onset of "siege warfare," a term that encompasses both attack and defense. It is pointless to apply

modern-day moral or ethical standards to the brutal and aggressive conduct of our ancestors, but it is interesting to observe that the main differences between then and now appear to be in the increasingly lethal, effective and widespread methods we use to secure our aims by aggression.

Until discoveries made in the twentieth century, it was thought that the practice of sophisticated fortification was developed first in medieval times. However, archaeology, a comparatively recent discipline, has shown that even in Neolithic times, towns were being fortified. Examples in Turkey and Mesopotamia reinforce the better-known discovery that by 5000 BC Jericho had been fortified in a way that would be familiar centuries later. Even then, it was not unknown to have projecting round towers built into walls in order to direct flanking fire from bows, spears and slings against attacking assailants. The many examples of hill forts in Europe (often erroneously called castles in Britain), although developed mainly during the Iron Age, are now thought to have originated even earlier.

As cities became ever larger and more powerful, forming the basis for states and empires, their defenses became increasingly more formidable in the face of attempts to assault and overcome them. By approximately 3000 BC Ur, the earliest civilization of which we have any extensive knowledge, had walls that were 80 to 110 feet (25 to 34m) thick at their bases. A culture that could produce the massive ziggurats of Sumeria could be expected to build similarly massive walls to protect them, and there is ample evidence to show that it was done. Ancient Egypt also built advanced fortifications, with crenellations (notched battlements) and machicolated balconies (with holes in the floor for dropping projectiles onto attackers). These were equal in

Previous pages: A wall fortress (Ming dynasty) at the western limit of the Great Wall of China, in Gansu Province. The Ming dynasty (founded in 1368) was the most active of the wall-builders in Chinese history. The first sight of civilization for travelers returning from the west, it is the world's largest manmade structure, some 1,600 miles (2,575 km) long.

Above: *The highly developed, fruitful agriculture of the fertile lands along the Nile made ancient Egypt an extremely tempting and profitable target for predatory nomadic tribes and other invaders. The African lands to the north—a source of Numidian slaves and ivory for frequent military forays— also served as a springboard for plundering attackers. The ancient Egyptians developed extremely sophisticated defenses to counter this threat, and some of their recently excavated fortresses equal medieval castles in effective design and construction.*

many respects to early-medieval patterns. Gatehouses provided with such intricacies as labyrinthine passages that forced the invader to turn his unshielded side toward the defender were also incorporated. The introduction of the use of chariots dictated the need for double doors for the sudden eruption of a sally, ensuring maximum surprise. However, the wider entrances increased the vulnerability of gatehouses, and this, in turn, required extra reinforcements, heralding the designs of medieval castles.

Archaeologists at Buhen, an elaborately fortified town on the Numidian border (now in the Sudan), unearthed a prime example of state-of-the-art Egyptian fortification. They were working there before the site disappeared under the waters of the great reservoir to be formed behind the Aswan High Dam. The fortress dated from between the twentieth and nineteenth centuries BC (XIIth Dynasty), and was constructed on the ruins of an even earlier fort.

Examples abound of great fortifications now being unearthed in Asia Minor and the Near East, but lack of space inhibits their description. However, mention must be made of the Hittites, who dominated Anatolia around 1650 BC, and were the master builders of the late Bronze Age. A wall 3.7 miles (6 km) long,

adapted cleverly to the changing levels of the land, protected their capital city of Hattusas. The walls tended to be circular, thus less easily undermined than those with rectangular corners. Underground posterns (back doors or gates) enabled surprise sallies, and, if necessary, a ready means of escape. A citadel was built on a hill within the city, and the city itself was divided into sections by interior walls to contain an enemy who had broken in. There was even a lower, outer wall, foretelling the outer walls of the concentric castles of the Middle Ages and the Byzantine defenses of Constantinople.

Probably the most famous of Bronze Age Anatolian fortresses, and surely the most excavated, is the multileveled Troy. Well known to us from Homer's *Iliad*, and Heinrich Schliemann's pioneering discoveries, Troy VI provides an excellent example of the main defensive architecture of its period. The walls consisted of a mud-brick superstructure built on a high stone rampart of well-worked masonry with a pronounced batter (backward slope) on its outer face. Again, there is a noticeable absence of acute corners, making hostile undermining more difficult and obviating the need for towers there to protect them: towers were then reserved to protect the gateways.

The struggles that brought about the rise and fall of great empires in the ancient world contributed to the steady evolution of ever-more-effective defenses, and, in turn, the development of means to overcome them. The foundation of the Assyrian state (around 1800 BC) and the Babylonian Empire (c. 1790) and their eventual collapse are witness to the ceaseless conflicts in the Near East, which continued uninterrupted until the advent of the *Pax Romana*. The arrival of the Israelites in their promised land (c. 1200 BC) provides us with more information about this formative era. Archaeological discoveries in the last century have revealed that many of the events recorded in the Old Testament, including intensive siege warfare carried out by and against the fortified towns of Judah and Israel, may well be accurate, although the account of the fall of the walls of Jericho (Joshua 6, 20–21) is widely considered at least partly symbolic and didactic. However, we are indebted to the Old Testament for some significant Rules of Engagement that have stood the test of time. Deuteronomy 20:

10 *When thou comest nigh unto a city to fight against it, then proclaim peace unto it.*
11 *And it shall be, if it make thee answer of peace, and open unto thee, then it shall be, that all the people that is found therein shall be tributaries unto thee, and they shall serve thee [involuntarily].*

12 *And if it will make no peace with thee, but will make war against thee, then thou shalt besiege it:*
13 *And when the Lord thy God hath delivered it unto thine hands, thou shalt smite every male thereof with the edge of the sword:*
14 *But the women, and the little ones, and the cattle, and all that is in the city, even all the spoil thereof, shalt thou take unto thyself [as booty]: and thou shalt eat [enjoy] the spoil of thine enemies, which the Lord thy God has given thee.*
15 *Thus shalt thou do unto all the cities which are very far off from thee, which are not of the cities of these nations.*
16 *But of the cities of these people, which the Lord thy God doth give thee for an inheritance, thou shalt save alive nothing that breatheth:*

There is no consensus on when and where certain parts of Deuteronomy were written, and indeed, who wrote them, but it

Below: The Byzantine fortress above the town of Simena, Turkey. The Byzantine Empire, the eastern continuation of the original Roman Empire, was under constant attack from "barbarians," and later, from expanding Muslim states. Impressive fortifications were developed, which were effective until the advent of Turkish attackers, particularly the Ottoman Turks. Bursa, near Istanbul, had been conquered by 1326, and most of Anatolia occupied by 1380. Istanbul, a Christian island in a Muslim world, held out until 1453.

Below: The Great Wall of China near Beijing. The early stages of this colossal endeavor were built in the third century BC, a first significant step in defending the boundary between nomadic horsemen and a culture based on domesticated animals and agriculture. A contemporary account describes the diverse weapons stored in each of the many crenellated towers: heavy crossbows, quivers of arrows, armor and helmets.

may be assumed that these rules were likely to have been generally accepted throughout all the evolving contemporary cultures, and were observed not only by the Israelites, but by warring factions throughout the Middle Ages and even later. These stipulations provide us with a deep insight into what siege warfare was all about: conquest and plunder on the part of the attacker, annihilation or slavery for the unsuccessful defender.

It is tempting to embark here on a study of ancient warfare, and to describe in detail the wars and sieges leading to the establishment of the Roman Empire. By then there were historians who could describe graphically the rise of the Greek states, and their internal wars and struggles with both Persia and Rome. The Punic wars with the Carthaginians, the rise of Macedonia and the breathtaking conquests of Alexander

the Great (356–23 BC) all provide fascinating examples of the development of fortifications, and the ensuing evolution of siege warfare. The Great Wall of China, although not in the direct line of descent of our medieval castles, deserves mention here since descriptions of it must have reached the ancient Near Eastern and Mediterranean worlds via the Silk Road (opened c. 112 BC), and could well have given the Romans a concept which led to the building, centuries later, of their great defensive barriers in northern England, Hadrian's Wall, and on the Rhine and Danube, the *limes* (borders).

WARFARE IN THE CLASSICAL WORLD

The first emperor of a united China started to incorporate earlier walls built around 300 BC for protection against the Huns raiding from the north into a single integrated system around 214 BC. The line of defense (essentially completed c. 1000 BC) extended 1,600 miles (2,575 km) from east to west—a complex system of walls, forts, towers and garrisons. It is highly significant to us inasmuch as it marked for the first time the boundary between steppe nomads and cultivated lands. Some authorities suggest that it was the initial success of this wall (which is the only manmade structure visible from the Moon) that caused the Huns to look to the west for plunder and slaves, which in turn drove the peoples who lived there, the Germanic folk, to move towards the west, the lands under Roman control.

And so we have come to a period wherein siege warfare reached its culmination. This was during the Roman Empire, before the start of the era known as the Dark Ages. The empire had its origins in c. 390 BC, when a Gallic invasion swept into Rome, then an embryonic city. This demonstrated

to Roman citizens the need for a more flexible and better-organized army, which led to the establishment of the legions. By AD 180 the Romans ruled the known civilized world, and, in the process, had attacked and overcome every known (and some were exceedingly strong) defensive system, while surviving attack by most of the states we now consider civilized, as well as continual conflict with the "barbarians" on their expanding borders. The builders, engineers, artillerymen and skilled artisans who figured in the establishment of every legion put their hard-earned experience to good effect. Certainly, the Romans would never have been able to forget the legendary devices produced to counter their attacks during the siege of Syracuse in 215 BC. They were up against one of the best scientific minds of all history—that of Archimedes, who produced a variety of effective stone-throwing engines (*petariæ*) to keep their fleet at a distance, and a gigantic claw that could reportedly seize a ship which had come against a wall, lift it into the air and then release it to sink, together with all the soldiers aboard. Archimedes was also credited with the invention of a long pivoted pole with a hooked end that could snatch an unsuspecting besieger into the air, and swing him into the city—probably to a nasty end. Besiegers, in turn, used this device, also called a claw, to capture unwary defenders.

The Romans are also responsible for the invention of the arch and of concrete. Both had a tremendous effect upon the strength and effectiveness of their fortifications and other buildings to this day, as discussed later when we consider the construction of castles. The remains of their massive walls, gateways and towers are still to be seen throughout Europe, North Africa and the Near East. In siegecraft, the Romans were demonstrably unsurpassed. One of their best-known sieges is that of the Palestinian fortress of Masada. Under their rulers, the Jews gained a reputation for being among the finest military architects of their era. Herod the Great had constructed a palatial castle in the newly rebuilt and strongly fortified Jerusalem about 24 BC, and his grandson Herod Agrippa improved these defenses some seventy years later. Their remains are still a source of wonder in Jerusalem. In AD 70, it took four Roman legions five months to overcome the defenses of Jerusalem. However, it is Masada that must be considered not only as an excellent example of a virtually impregnable castle, but also of the determination, perseverance and outstanding military skills of the Romans. This fortress can well be called a castle, since Herod the Great constructed it about 30 BC purely as a refuge for himself, his family and his retainers. It stands on a plateau on top of a high hill that has precipitous sides, west of the Dead Sea. The fortress on top is accessible only by a narrow winding path, and the plateau was surrounded by a massive stone curtain wall some 12 feet (9.4m) thick and 18 feet (5.5m) high. There were thirty-eight towers, 75 feet (23m) high, spaced along the walls, and a strong keep commanded the approach path. Another tower was built lower down the path to act as an outpost—the forerunner of the barbican. The keep was very much on the lines of a medieval stone keep: rectangular in shape, with a tower at each corner some 90 feet (30.5m) high. Huge cisterns to hold rainwater were cut into the rock and vast stores of provisions laid down.

Herod did not have occasion to seek refuge in his castle himself. However, upon the destruction of Jerusalem in AD 70, a group of Jewish Zealots (as they were

Below: The Hospitallers, the last Crusaders, were driven from Acre, their final foothold in the Holy Land, in 1291. They withdrew to Cyprus, but had conquered the island of Rhodes by 1309. There they built massive defenses that formed a bulwark against repeated Ottoman Turkish attacks until 1522, when the island fell to Suleyman I, the Magnificent. The Hospitallers' magnificent castle in Rhodes reflects a period of transition in castle design: the decline of the typical medieval building and the beginning of the artillery fort.

called) held out here against a besieging Roman force. In the well-justified expectation of a long struggle to destroy them, in AD 73 the besiegers first built a stone wall around the foot of the hill, strengthened by forts at intervals, to ensure that there could be no reinforcement and no escape. This *circumvallation* was the standard siege practice by this time, as used by the Romans against Vercingetorix in Gaul in 52 BC, for example, and later employed throughout the Middle Ages.

Since the walls of the castle, perched on its crag, were out of the range of his siege engines, the Roman commander built a huge mound, surmounted by an iron-clad tower, facing the main gate. From this, he could bring down effective fire on the battlements and deter the Zealots from preventing construction of a huge ramp up to the walls. A large battering ram could then be dragged up, which completely overthrew a portion of the wall. The defenders managed to block the gap with an earth-and-timber structure. When this, in turn, was destroyed by fire, the Zealots realized that nothing now could save them and their families from the horrendous torture and agonizing deaths for which the Romans were notorious. They slaughtered their women and children and committed mass suicide.

This siege has been described in some detail because it is well documented and provides a graphic background for the following discussion of siege warfare. Roman methodology and weaponry had changed so little between the downfall of their empire and the methods used against castles throughout the Middle Ages that it is well nigh impossible to date these conflicts accurately. The greatest difference was probably in the resources in manpower,

weaponry and logistics available to the besieger, so we may consider siege warfare in general as developed by the Romans and carried on throughout the violent period preceding their medieval successors.

Before that, however, it will be interesting to take a look at the fortifications the Romans built to defend the farthermost limits of their empire, since these also had a great influence when castles were being built again. The great fortresses built as garrisons near major cities, and the walls surrounding them, were initially to protect the Romans from uprisings in the newly conquered territories and to serve as deterrents. The frontier defenses were different: they were designed to hinder an encroaching raider until a strong force could be mustered from a supporting garrison fort or fortified town. Originally, they consisted mainly of a wooden palisade and ditch, but they were successively strengthened with stone walls when threats became more acute or time allowed. The professional soldier will recognize the need to keep troops occupied and trained when stationed in remote regions far from home, and what better than a spell of wall-, or castle-building! The best-known protected boundaries are Hadrian's Wall, built to keep the "barbarian" Scots out of a relatively civilized England, and the Limes, a fortified area that stretched for 2,500 miles (4,000 km) along the Rhine and Danube to the Black Sea, to protect the eastern and northern borders. The Limes, of course, could not match the much shorter Hadrian's Wall, which was a concentrated, integrated defensive system, with stone mile castles, signal towers (beacons to signal an attack), forts every 5 miles (8 km) and turrets every 540 yards (494m). It extended for 80 miles (129 km), utilizing the natural defensive features of the landscape to excellent effect.

The forts built to defend England against the depredations of the seaborne Saxon raiders, under the command of a general called the Count of the Saxon Shore, are of particular interest to later developments. Positioned to defend ports and estuaries, they often formed the basis for subsequent Norman castles. Pevensey, for example, can boast of being a Norman and later a medieval castle (prison for England's Henry V's stepmother), an Elizabethan gun emplacement, and in World War II, a machine-gun post! The weakening of Rome's hold over the empire, its internal disputes and the withdrawal of the legions made it impossible for these defenses to be adequately manned, and in the fifth century the western Roman Empire was finally swamped by invading Visigoths, Ostrogoths, Alans and Vandals (who also reached North Africa), Jutes, Angles and Saxons, Frisians, Franks, Burgundians, the Suivi and the Lombards, who settled on the lands they had conquered. The Allemani ("all men") were a coalition of many Germanic tribes, and *Allemand* is what the present-day French still call the Germans.

It will be noted from the preceding paragraph that it was the western part of the Roman Empire that was overrun and occupied by the "barbarians." The eastern part had broken away from the west not long after (AD 395) the Emperor Constantine had built the magnificent walled city of Constantinople (now Istanbul) on the Bosphorus. This guarded the narrow straits between the Mediterranean and the Black Sea. Byzantium, as this half of the empire came to be called, sat astride the major trade routes between east and west, and was very much the richest half of the empire, in terms of produce, trade and culture. It encompassed the legendary cities of

Alexandria and Cairo, Damascus, the wealthy Hellenistic cities on the shores of the Mediterranean and Greece itself. The Armenians, a race of expert castle builders, were either an integral part of the Byzantine Empire, or neighbors and allies. Its importance to the story of castle building is that here the traditions of the "old" Roman Empire could continue uninterrupted, and be reinforced by the hard lessons learned in the constant struggles with predatory neighbors. The major enemy were the Persians, until the increasing power of the Saracens and other militant desert nomads was spurred on by their conversion to the Muslim faith. The empire was insulated to some extent from the ravages of the Goths, Slavs and Huns on the north and west by quasi-allied neighbors, and the Danube

again became a useful barrier. The fact that Byzantium had developed its own brand of Christianity (Orthodox/Greek, rather than Roman Catholic/Latin) was significant centuries later in the time of the Crusaders, but until that time it was able to adopt and develop many methods of siege warfare that were essentially of Eastern origin, and which we shall be looking at later. During the reign of Justinian (527–565), who is regarded as one of the greatest military engineers of all time, some 700 fortifications were rebuilt or constructed in the empire. To quote an acknowledged expert on fortification, Sidney Toy: "It was largely to the scientific and powerful works then built, many of which still exist, that the mediæval military engineer, both Christian and Saracen, owed his inspiration."

SIEGE WARFARE

Having now reached the first summit of achievement in the evolution of fortifications, it may be worthwhile to look next at the methods and means that were developed, step-by-step, in attempts to overcome them. We will explore detailed defensive designs when we consider the construction of a castle in some detail in a later chapter. Let us now take as an example a strong, well-defended castle seen through the eyes of an attacker at some indeterminate period before the advent of the cannon.

First of all, the attacking commander had to assess the location of the castle he intended to seize. Castles were positioned to make maximum use of all natural features. Crags, cliffs and escarpments were the preferred sites, since they made access under a hail of missiles extremely difficult, if not impossible. Such a location could neutralize the effect of siege engines by rendering them out of range or impossible to access unless, as with Masada, the

Below: Exultant, hard-pressed Christian defenders of a besieged Crusader castle welcome the long-awaited arrival of a strong relieving force, led by a bishop and chanting priests. Note the trebuchet on the strong platform, designed to withstand the shockwaves generated when it was discharged.

Strategic Siting

Dunnottar Castle, Grampian, Scotland (above), is protected on all sides by great cliffs. Little now remains of the original twelfth-century building, and the L-shaped tower house seen here dates from the fourteenth century. Below, Gutenfels Castle, perched high above the town of Kaub, on the Rhine, built in the first half of the thirteenth century, overlooks the fourteenth-century Pfalzgrafstein Castle, which was ideally sited to levy tolls.

Page 24: Burg Katz, a late fourteenth-century castle, protects St. Goarshausen directly below, providing an ideal view of the famed Lorelei. Overleaf, castles surrounded by water: Castle Stalker, Strathclyde, a fine example of a tower house, stands on an island in Loch Laich, near Oban, Scotland, and resembles Eilean Donan (gatefold) built in 1220 on a rocky island in Loch Duich, Highlands, to protect against Viking raids.

attacker had the time and resources to build ramps and very high towers on which to set up his batteries. Similarly, a position on lakes, rivers or the sea meant that siege engines could not be brought within range. Additionally, a castle on the coast of the sea, a river or some other wide stretch of water could often be reinforced and resupplied by boat, if the besieger did not have an adequate navy. In low-lying land, a moat, or deep dry ditch with sheer sides, could also prevent the siting of siege engines nearby, and, as an extra advantage, make mining, boring and sapping so difficult as to obviate their use. To prevent a surprise assault and provide a clear field of fire, the ground surrounding the walls would be completely cleared of bushes, trees and undergrowth. Location on a narrow promontory or spur could avoid the necessity for defending three sides of a rectangular building as heavily as the fourth, as well as making access extremely difficult.

At this point, having appreciated the physical difficulties ahead of him, the commander would ask himself why the castle had been built where it was. What was its main purpose, and could this be neutralized without an outright assault? What was the main aim of the besieger? Could this be achieved by devastating the surrounding lands and villages, causing economic ruin for the defender? The English Black Prince (Edward, Prince of Wales) had had a great success with this method (his *chevauchée*) in 1355. Was his own operation part of a wider strategic move, and subject to the overriding orders of his lord? By penning the defenders inside their castle, could they be prevented from making attacks on the invader's own lines of supply, or going to the assistance of a neighboring castle or town? If there was good intelligence about the enemy's logistical situation, he could possibly assess who was likely to starve first, the defend-

Below: Caerlaverock Castle, on the coast southeast of Dumfries, Scotland, was built in the late thirteenth century. It is almost unique, being triangular in ground plan, with two sides protected by an arm of the sea and the third by a wide moat. In the wars of independence with the English, Edward I laid siege to it in 1300; after four more successive sieges, it was finally "slighted" (destroyed) by the Scots in 1312 to prevent the English from reoccupying it. It was rebuilt in the fifteenth century and provided with the great gatehouse and gun ports.

ers or the besiegers. How good were the defenders' water supplies and his own? For a Crusader in the Holy Land, for example, this factor would loom very large. Could a relieving force attack him? How long before they could arrive? King John of England rescued his mother, Eleanor of Aquitaine, from the clutches of his nephew, Arthur of Brittany, in 1202. Having received the news of her danger when he was in Le Mans, he immediately set off on a 100-mile (160 km) dash over rudimentary roads to reach her castle in Mirabeau forty-eight hours later. He completely surprised her kidnappers at breakfast, and captured more than 200 knights and six barons with hardly a struggle. Arthur himself was put in the bag, and Eleanor released from the keep where she had been confined.

An experienced commander would want to find out about the morale of the defenders, their numbers and weaponry, and to interrogate spies, traitors, peasants and prisoners (no Geneva Convention to flout) about every aspect of the castle and its garrison. He would then, carefully and objectively, in the light of his own strengths and weaknesses, make an appreciation and plan. The courses open to him would probably be either to move quietly away or to besiege the castle. If the latter, he would then decide either to attack as soon as possible with all available resources and methods, or to avoid an all-out assault and attempt to starve out the defenders. (The English Duke of Bedford made the disastrous decision to do just this in 1492, setting the stage for Jeanne d'Arc's dramatic rescue of Orléans.) Since sieges could last for years, he would almost certainly have thought first about gaining the castle either by stealth or trickery, with the Trojan Horse as an example. The fact

Right: San Marino, with its fortified abbey in the walled city, was near enough to the Adriatic coast to merit strong fortification against pirates and invaders. The Ottoman Turks reached the Adriatic in 1371, but never gained a firm foothold in Italy: a landing at Otranto failed due to internal dynastic strife. San Marino, built on Mt. Titana, 2,650 feet (800m) high, became a republic in 1862. It proclaimed neutrality in World War II, but after invasion by the Wehrmacht, declared war on Germany on September 23, 1944. San Marino claims to be the oldest state in Europe and one of the smallest in the world.

that he was making the assessment at all would indicate that any chance of surprising his enemy had failed.

Froissart, a contemporary medieval historian, gives a graphic account of how a castle was seized without bloodshed. He tells how the "captain" of a castle was taken prisoner one night in the neighboring town while boozing there ("making

Below: "*The lady who saw herself in a hard case, saw she was not able to make war herself, for saving of her husband's life she yielded up the castle.*"

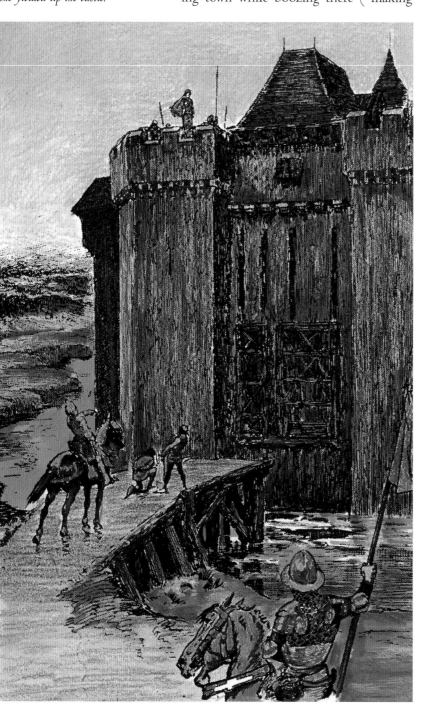

cheer together") with some merchants from Carcassonne, a fortified medieval town in southern France. The next morning his captor, a knight rather less chivalrous than the ideal, paraded him in front of his castle and told his wife that her husband would be beheaded unless she surrendered. "The lady," says Froissart, "who saw herself in a hard case, saw she was not able to make war herself, for saving of her husband's life she yielded up the castle." The winner held the castle for five years. Having completely pillaged the surrounding countryside and towns for a distance of five leagues (about 15 miles, or 24 km), he sold it, together with a neighboring castle he had captured by cunning, for "eight thousand francs," and retired to Lourdes, his main base. As Froissart sums it up: "So thus in this manner of adventure knights did put themselves daily."

Having decided on an assault, our commander would then have to make preparations. Anticipating that this could take considerable time, he would build a defensive palisade and ditch around the castle. This could well be facing both inward, to prevent escape or sallies, and outward, to ward off an attack by a relieving force. He would also fortify his own camp. If there were a moat or ditch round the target, this would have to be filled in by fascines (bundles of sticks) or bridged by his men. To protect them from the missiles fired from the walls, and rocks and fire hurled onto them, he would build a cat, or mobile penthouse, for every location to be assaulted. These were long, one-story structures, constructed of stout timbers and covered with dampened rawhides. Mounted on wheels, they were propelled forward by the men inside, over the moat, and right up to the walls. While this was going on, the commander would keep up a barrage of arrows and missiles from those siege engines that he could bring to bear. The longbow was the preferred weapon here, since an archer could loose five well-aimed arrows against the battlements in the time it took for a crossbowman to fire one bolt. Slingshots were in use on either side. Great accuracy could be obtained, and there was always a plentiful supply of ammunition. David had shown that even a Goliath was not proof against a well-aimed stone. Archers would be protected by mantlets or pavises—wooden shields that were either held up by a supporter, or fixed in the ground. The defenders would probably have used cross-bows, if they had them. These, although they had a slower rate of fire, had a longer range, approximately 375 yards (340m) compared to 220 yards (201m) and their heavier bolts, greater penetration. Arguably, they were more accurate, but that is a debate best left to the aficionados.

While all this was in progress, the commander would be positioning his artillery. Depending on relative heights and distance, he might build a high mound on which to place his siege weapons, as in the siege of Masada. Whatever their location, he would have to build wooden defenses to protect them and their operators from the enemy's artillery. Ideally, while his would be out of range, he could neutralize theirs. He may have had to manufacture his siege weapons on the spot, especially the very large ones, and he would have engineers, blacksmiths and carpenters to do this, given an adequate supply of suitable nearby trees to be felled. In one of the Ancient Greek battles, the invaders were forced to break up their ships to obtain an adequate supply of timber for this purpose. The Romans had catapults mounted on strong horse-drawn carts, and the well-prepared medieval warrior would have had the same.

The siege engines themselves had evolved over the years from Roman times, basically keeping the same designs, but improving in accuracy, range and weight of missile. Most of our descriptions of ancient weaponry are of Roman artillery, depictions of which grace the triumphal columns and arches erected by victorious emperors to impress their people. Roman authors often give details of the weaponry used by both sides in their descriptions of battles and sieges. Projectile-hurling engines can be divided roughly into three categories, all depending upon the tension provided by springs, thongs, or twisted ropes. A later invention was the tremendously powerful trebuchet, which operated by means of a counterweight and considerable leverage, or a strong team of soldiers pulling down violently on the short end, jerking it. In fact, Archimedes could have invented this, but he didn't!

Above: The unusual hexagonal tower of Raglan Castle, in southeast Wales, was built on the site of an earlier castle of the late eleventh century by William ap Thomas, who had fought beside Henry V at Agincourt in 1415. Built of pale gold stone, it was called the Yellow Tower of Gwent. Thomas's son, the Earl of Pembroke, extended it and added luxurious living quarters and the great gatehouse.

Right: The trebuchet, probably invented by the Chinese and further developed in the Middle East, was one of the most significant factors in the evolution of castle design until the siege cannon. Encountered by Europeans during the Crusades, it was quickly adopted. Richard the Lionheart used one with devastating effect at the siege of Acre (1189–91). The trebuchet became the major weapon of both defense and attack in siege warfare. It could hurl huge round stones some 200–300 yards (180–275m) in a high trajectory and with great accuracy. In the hands of a skilled artilleryman, it could destroy walls by repeated impact at the same spot. Tall towers were particularly vulnerable.

Petrariæ (as the name suggests) could fling huge rocks weighing some 110 pounds (50 kg) over about 540 yards (500m); ballistæ, mangonels, or onagars threw stones of about 55 pounds (25 kg) several hundred yards; catapults, or scorpions, cast smaller stones, lead weights, bolts, or darts, and, most important, firebrands. At the siege of Acre (1189–91, during the Crusades) the king of France had an engine that, after constant pounding, broke down the massive city wall. In this same siege, the king of England, Richard the Lionheart, used an engine that killed twelve men with one shot. Stone balls, when they crashed into a wall, broke into many splinters, each capable, like shrapnel, of causing a terrible wound. These could well have been trebuchets, which, until the Crusades, were unknown in the West, like so many other aspects of warfare. It is thought that the trebuchet originated in China, was developed further by the Arabs and played a very important part in the Crusades and all

siege warfare thereafter. The cannon finally superseded it some two centuries later, marking the decline of the castle's effectiveness. The Byzantines had discovered Greek fire, a form of the modern napalm, with similar characteristics. It could be projected by a siege engine and was used to great effect against the Saracens, finally defeating a formidable attack against Constantinople (Istanbul) that had lasted from 668 to 675, and another determined attack in 716, destroying their fleet with its aid. The Saracens learned how to make it and used it with devastating effect against the Crusaders. The secret of its composition has now been lost, but it is thought that it was used in medieval Europe.

The next decision to be made by the attacker was how to gain entry into the castle. There were several possibilities: to make an assault over the walls; to break through the walls or through the gate; to cause them to collapse by undermining or sapping, or to gain direct entry by tunneling. To assault over the walls was probably the speediest course if one could achieve surprise, possibly by night. He could use long scaling ladders, which normally had a large hook at the extremity. He could also use flexible ladders fashioned of rope or leather, which could be thrown over the wall like a grappling iron. The success of such a method would depend upon the height of the walls, the number of experienced men of high caliber he could call upon and the strength and determination of the defenders. For this kind of assault, a siege tower, known as a belfry, was a common, less risky, method, which had been in use since 200 or 300 BC, if not earlier. The tower was built of stout timbers, several stories high, and covered in dampened rawhides to prevent its being set on fire—a threat greatly feared. It was mounted on wheels, and could be propelled right up to the walls, where it towered above the battlements, allowing the archers to pour arrows down onto the defenders below. Twelfth-century towers were recorded as being between 150 and 300 feet (45 to 95m) high. Loopholes at each story allowed covering fire to be directed at the enemy archers. A drawbridge was finally let down onto the summit of the wall or tower being attacked, enabling the hand-picked, well-armored assault force to rush down onto the battlements and swarm into the castle, slaying the opposition with swords, axes and maces. At least, that was the plan, but like all plans, it often went badly awry. The expression *malvoisin* (bad neighbor)

seems to have had several meanings. It was the name given to the trebuchet that was used to such good (or bad, depending on what side of the walls you were on) effect at the siege of Acre. It was also used of a siege tower or belfry, and it could describe an earthen mound built to provide a higher level for archers and artillery. It could even denote a complete castle, fully and permanently manned to inhibit that of a threatening subordinate. The Middle Ages were pervaded by very well-justified paranoia. In those days there were no standardizing authorities for nomenclature except, perhaps, the Church. Edward I of England called *his* trebuchet, built to overcome a Scottish castle, "Warwolf"!

Below: Conwy (1283–87), seen here from the site of its former drawbridge, is one of the magnificent castles built by Edward I to subjugate the Welsh. Designed by Edward's master builder, James of St. George, it was the costliest of all Edward's Welsh castles, notable for its eight great circular towers, three gateways and spacious great hall.

Probably the best-known siege weapon is the battering ram, used to create a breach through which to make an assault. This consisted of a substantial tree trunk, slung within a wooden housing, mounted on wheels and covered with dampened rawhides. In later centuries iron plates were also used. The ram was tipped with a heavy iron head, and swung repeatedly against the wall or gate to be breached. A crew could number more than fifty men, who would join in the general assault once a breach had been achieved. An alternative was the bore, similar to the ram, but with a pointed head, so that it could pick away at the stonework and so cause the wall to collapse. Defenders would attempt to neutralize the effects of these engines by lowering mattresses at the point of impact, or by hooking the head with a grappling device and tipping it over.

There were two similar methods of causing a wall or tower to collapse. The easiest, but most dangerous, was to dig a pit at the base and directly under the wall to undermine it. This alone might succeed in bringing a wall down, but normally it would be necessary to shore up the pit, fill it with combustible material and set fire to it. When the shoring collapsed, so did the wall. Much later, gunpowder would have been used. Against a weak defense, it might be possible to pick away at the stonework with crowbars, under cover of a "cat," until it collapsed.

A far more sophisticated method of undermining, which took much longer, was to tunnel. This method was recorded as long ago as 211 BC and was probably even older. A tunnel was dug from a safe location to a spot directly under a wall. It was then shored up, as in the previous method, filled with brushwood and set on fire. Sometimes the tunnelers added

slaughtered pigs to the pyre, so that their melting fat could increase its intensity. It was certainly not unknown for a direct entry to the castle's interior to be gained by tunneling, in an effort to surprise the garrison. The defenders used bowls of water set on the ground and watched closely to detect surface vibrations caused by digging. There is a record of thin plates of brass being used by the ancients for the same purpose. Once tunneling had been detected, the defenders would build a counter-mine. The aim of this was either to break into the enemy's tunnel, which would lead to a desperate underground battle, or to smoke him out. Defenders against a Roman siege are known to have used a large container full of smoldering feathers. The Welsh were noted miners, and this gives credence to Shakespeare's portrayal of Captain Fluellen (a stereotypical Welshman) as a redoubtable soldier in *The Life of Henry the Fifth*.

This has been a very short summary of the factors a commander would consider in making his initial appreciation, before making final decisions: most of the basic elements would be much the same irrespective of when these were made. It also gives us some insight into the design decisions faced by the castle builder. The assessment of the situation required by the captain of an attacking force highlights the value of a castle as a deterrent. If a commander faced with a siege did not do this carefully, with the advice of experts in the various methods to be employed, he faced heavy losses in men and material, and unnecessary delays. He could be facing an absolute disaster. It was a grave decision, and it is interesting to note that the odds were often in favor of the besieged. In this respect, a well-designed, stoutly built and stoutly defended castle was a force multiplier, enabling defenders to repulse successfully forces at least ten times as strong, or to delay an attack beyond a profitable limit. Therefore, we can understand the practice of what could be called "siege poker." While the attacker was making his appreciation, so was the defender, even more carefully, for he had more to lose if defeated. The stakes were very high, possibly life or death for him and his family, and almost certain death, or worse, for his soldiers. Before the first arrow was fired, the besieger would offer terms (echoes of Deuteronomy). Normally, these would be along the following lines: if the captain would surrender his castle, he would be allowed to march out with his entire garrison, their dependents and possessions, all completely unharmed. The defender would have considered this very carefully, and a major factor beyond the purely military concerns would be his own morale and that of his garrison. His own loyalty to whatever cause he served, and that of his men to him, would be assessed. The chances of relief, reinforcement and resupply would be examined, together with the overall logistic system. An outright refusal of these demands might then result in their being adjusted and ameliorated.

If the castle was not relieved by a certain time, it would then be surrendered, probably on less advantageous terms. The answer could well depend upon the faith the defender put in his God, his lord or his allies. Sadly, thousands were slaughtered for minute deviations from formal religious beliefs. Terms could be offered, and accepted or not, at different stages in the siege, depending on progress. Terror was often used to sway a garrison to capitulate, and there is no shortage of accounts of prisoners being flayed alive in front of the defenders on the walls. Other frightful sto-

ries over the ages include the amputation of limbs, and blinding. The heads of captured defenders were often projected into a besieged castle. In many cases, the attacker offered to lift the siege after a period if certain requirements were met by the defender. It should also be remembered that both besieged and besieger, cramped closely together, were under constant threat of bubonic plague and similar contagious diseases, often fostered by the hurling of rotting animal carcasses over the walls. This, however, is where we risk departing from the purely military and become involved in the wider disciplines of history, psychology, epidemiology and theology.

Below: A detail of the impressive gatehouse of central England's Warwick Castle, viewed from the courtyard inside the eastern wall. The castle stands on the site of an early motte-and-bailey castle on a cliff above the River Avon; most of the surviving structure dates from the fourteenth century.

THE FIRST CASTLES

The steady development of fortress design and construction seems to have stagnated in the lands of the western Roman Empire after they were occupied by the Germanic peoples. Although they adopted many Roman customs and traditions, fortress building was not one of them. Apparently, they were content to depend upon the strong defenses left to them by the Romans, although they probably lacked and missed the experience of the veteran legionnaires who had once manned them. It has been suggested that many of the folk and fairy tales we enjoy today include stories of giants because they were credited with the many and varied massive stone structures the Romans had built throughout Europe. The Germanic establishment of diverse kingdoms and dukedoms destroyed the centralized government that had so benefited the Romans until their decline. The standardized "Operational Procedures" evident in every aspect of the legions' activities ensured that even a mediocre leader could achieve a satisfactory solution to most problems. Even Charlemagne's few military castles were designed on Roman models.

However, this was a far from peaceful time. All Europe was under constant attack by Saracens, Magyars, Vikings, Normans, Jutes, Saxons, Angles and Danes. The peoples abandoned by the Romans tried to make shift with the fortifications they had left behind, with no obvious success. The invaders themselves were forced to build fortified refuges to protect themselves not only from original inhabitants, but from other marauders, and from successive waves of roving predators. The Normans overran northern and western France so speedily that any surviving Roman forts obviously did not impede them. This was the period when the legendary King Arthur fought his equally legendary battles with the invading Saxons or other Teutonic or Scandinavian tribes. His castles and Knights of the Round Table were not conjured into a purely literary existence for several centuries. This was an age of pitched battles, of shield walls and wild assaults on them with battleax, sword and arrow.

Fortifications consisted mainly of earthworks, wooden palisades and ditches. History started to repeat itself when Alfred the Great of England and his children built *burhs* (fortified towns) to defend their citizens from the Danes, and similar defensive measures were being taken all over Europe. It is interesting to note that many English place names end in "burgh," reflecting their Germanic origins, while the suffixes "-caster" and "-chester" often boast of Roman origin. The same applies in many (other) countries, where the endings "-kastel" and "-castel," or "-berg" and "-burg," indicate a probable Roman or Germanic origin, respectively.

The origins of the true castle, as defined in the introduction, can be traced back to the time of Charlemagne, the great Frankish warrior and king (742–814), who conquered and ruled most of what we now call Europe, except for most of Iberia (present-

day Spain and Portugal), which had been conquered and occupied by the Moors. He was a firm and sometimes ruthless ruler, renowned for slaughtering 4,000 Saxons as an inducement for the remainder to convert to Christianity. It is understandable that the pope, seeking to secure his own position, crowned him as the first Emperor of the Romans, endowing the office with a spiritual aura and starting the often strained and fluctuating relationship between Church and sectarian ruler that would mark the history of Europe for centuries to come. It should also be borne in mind that the Romans had never occupied most of Northern Europe west of the Rhine, and traces of massive Saxon earthen ramps, palisades and ditches have survived as evidence of the epic struggles for mastery between Frank and Saxon.

Charlemagne's empire was vast, and to control it he had to appoint trusty supporters to settle in all these regions and govern on his behalf. They were well-tried military leaders who were granted huge tracts of land in return for their loyalty, and mandated to provide him with military and financial backing at need. This was the start of the feudal system, which was the basis of government in Europe for centuries and introduced into England by the Norman king William the Conqueror in 1066. The noblemen—"Lords" (from the Saxon *loaf ward*, person in authority), "Dukes" (Latin *dux*, leader), or "Counts" (Latin *comes*, office-bearer)—in turn divided their lands into estates that they entrusted to their followers, who were required to provide military assistance in return. This implied that at every level of the chain of government, an adequate retinue of trained and well-equipped soldiers was established and equipped for war. The magnate could well be a bishop (often a close blood relation of the ruler or

influential noble) who had his own subordinates: they too owed him military service in return for a grant of land. Some bishops bore the responsibilities of secular princes, charged with defending the borders of the land against aggression. The Continental equivalent of the English "knight" (derived from Old English/Saxon *cniht*, a servant) was *chevalier* (mounted soldier) or *Ritter*, terms used respectively in Romance-language, or German-speaking areas. At first, not all these appointments were hereditary, being rewards for faithful service, but as feudalism developed, with "vassals" paying homage to their lord for their "fief," and vowing loyalty, they rapidly became so, with the exception, of course, of bishops. This accounts for the *von*, *de* and *of* included in the aristocratic surnames and titles of the time, and still often jealously preserved today. It is a sad reflection on human nature that these vows were obeyed as scrupulously as marriage vows.

The other significant step toward the development of a medieval society dominated by castles was a revolution in warfare. The horse had long played an important military role, either pulling war-chariots or providing the Huns and other steppe-dwelling predatory nomads with speed and mobility. The Romans employed auxiliary cavalry on their borders. These were often horse-mounted archers, who could be useful in pursuit, or in harassing a retreating enemy, but not in a frontal assault. The invention of stirrups changed this. Using these, a mounted warrior had a firm seat on his horse and could wield his sword more safely. Most importantly, he could hold a lance securely under his arm and charge an enemy headlong.

This soon revolutionized warfare in Europe, since few could withstand the shock of a concentrated attack by heavily armored men. A document of 981 reveals that the Holy Roman Emperor of that time (Otto II) could call on 2,000 mailed knights from among his immediate vassals. But in a land split up into warring factions, where alliances could change overnight, a knight could lose the favor of his lord for the smallest misdemeanor, and a lord incur the wrath of his ruler for plotting to overthrow him—or even being suspected of it, since a well-justified atmosphere of insecurity prevailed. A troop of mounted men-at-arms could appear without warning outside the palace of a prince or nobleman, and if he was fortunate, eject him and his family— if not, murder him, or cart him off in chains for trial. The leader of the attackers could well be the man to whom the estates had already been granted.

Hence the need for a stout defense against a fast-moving mounted enemy, and soon the castle appeared in all the lands. There was another cause, too, for the pervasive insecurity: the lord of a newly granted estate in a "foreign" land recently seized by a neighboring duke wanted to sleep securely at night. His peasants, serfs or villeins, on whose labors the prosperity of the estate depended, and whom he often taxed beyond the limits of survival, could easily murder him and his family in an assault under cover of darkness. The Saxon thane could feel secure in his dwelling, usually surrounded by well-wishing villagers, but this did not apply to the Norman landlord in, say, southern Italy, Sicily or England. Another urgent requirement for a defended base was to protect the horses. Not only was a war-horse (*destrier*) thirty times as expensive as a normal hack, the knight's power to exercise authority over his lands, and to defend them, was largely dependent upon the fact that he and his followers were mounted. Thus even the early forms of feudalism brought the necessity for an imposing and powerfully forti-

fied residence. The castle dominated one's lands and effectively proclaimed (in modern parlance): "Don't even think about it!"

There are traces of early, very simple, castles to be found in both France and Germany. Not all were built of earth and wood, though most seem to have consisted of an oval enclosure formed by a ditch and a bank. Evidence of this is found in edicts of Charles the Bald, king of France. In 862 he ordered defenses constructed to resist the invading Normans (probably Danes), who were invading the north coast. However, the resulting proliferation of castles threatened his own authority, and in 864 he issued another edict, mandating the demolition of all fortresses that had been built without his royal license. However, five years later he had to fortify all towns between the Loire and the Seine Rivers again.

The Normans, once sea-borne invaders, soon established themselves in northern France as vassals of the king. They were granted the Duchy of Normandy in 911, contingent upon their becoming Christians, and soon became adept castle builders. The Frankish king who made this agreement was Charles the Simple! Fortifications against the incursions of Slavs and Magyars were being developed continually in Germany. The Counts of Anjou, who owed nominal suzerainty to the French king, but like most counts and dukes in France at that time were virtually autonomous, built a chain of castles that split the lands of a rival, the Count of Blois, in two. One of these, at Langeais (Inde-et-Loire), is thought to be the earliest example of a stone castle in France built before 995, and served as a model for later buildings. A rectangular donjon (keep), it is remarkably similar to the great stone keeps that the Normans constructed later in England, Ireland and Italy, as described in the following chapter.

Copying good, or successful, design was quite as common in the Middle Ages as it is today. The ever-present threat to southern France from the Muslim invaders in Iberia encouraged fortifications there and saw the emergence of the Carolingian dynasty. Charles Martel (of the epic Song of Roland) defeated the Arab armies at Poitiers in 732, and his son, Pepin III, was the father of Charlemagne, who, as we have seen, started it all with the emergence of the feudal system.

It is not possible to generalize about the construction of early castles, but by the turbulent eleventh century a type known as the motte-and-bailey had become the most successful. It is thought that Edward I's Norman favorites (his mother was a Norman princess) built this type of castle to guard the lands he had granted them. They were certainly unpopular enough in their new homeland. The Bayeux Tapestry clearly illustrates many of these castles in Normandy and neighboring duchies, two being of particular sig-

nificance. One portion of the tapestry shows the surrender of Dinan by the Duke of Brittany to Duke William of Normandy, with two knights engaged in setting fire to the wooden tower (a weakness we shall look at later). The other famous illustration is of the Normans building their castle at Hastings, to give themselves a firm base before the battle of 1066. Some authors believe that this had been prefabricated in Normandy and shipped across the Channel with the invaders in specially built ships. The basic motte-and-bailey consisted of an artificial mound of earth, built up from soil thrown from a surrounding ditch, or a natural hillock with the sides made steeper. There are some indications that this mound was often composed of successive layers of stones, clay and earth to provide stability, and modern excavations reveal various methods. Peasants could probably be persuaded to lend a hand with the digging, if they wished to avoid being flogged. The mound

Above: The earliest castles in Europe were the motte-and-bailey type. These were built quickly with the labor of impressed local peasants. The motte was a mound of earth with steep sides and a flat summit, which was surrounded by a loopholed wooden palisade. A battlemented wooden tower inside this palisade was the residence of the lord and his family. A wide, deep ditch surrounded the base of the motte, providing much of the material from which it was constructed. The area around the motte was called the bailey (sometimes there were two), which was ringed with another wooden palisade having an internal platform for the defenders, and a further ditch.

would be between some 50 feet and 120 feet (15–35m) high, and the flat top between 50 feet and 300 feet (15–90m) across. The surrounding ditch would be filled either with water (forerunner of the moat) or with sharpened staves. A wooden palisade was built between the ditch and the base of the mound, and a one- or two-story wooden edifice constructed on the summit. Another wooden palisade was built around the summit, enclosing the castle. A wooden gatehouse and possibly an early form of drawbridge guarded the entrance, and a step path guarded by a fortified gate led to a tower, which was the accommodation of the lord, his family, retainers and stores. The land enclosed by the lower palisade was known as the bailey, and was as large, or small, as required. Some castles even had two baileys, but this was exceptional. The bailey was used to corral the horses and cattle, and to hold store huts for fodder and probably the cookhouse. In France, the bailey was known as the poultry yard, for obvious reasons!

The great advantage of this type of castle was that it could be constructed with great speed from material usually at hand, and it did not require skills beyond those of an experienced soldier. This was of the essence in a land newly conquered, where a counterattack could be expected from the defeated enemy, or guerrilla-type harassment from the defeated population. The great disadvantage was that the wooden structures could easily be set on fire, by flaming arrows or firebrands. There is some evidence that the woodwork was plastered with clay to help prevent this, with very vulnerable positions like the gatehouse being protected with dampened rawhides. As part of the psychological warfare then practiced, the whole structure was painted white, a practice that was continued for centuries. This was a challenge to an attacker to do

his worst, and a constant reminder to the subject peasants of who was boss.

The siting of these early castles—often still seen today, if only as an overgrown hump in the landscape—has to be fully appreciated. When the three- or four-story wooden tower on the summit was completed, it provided an excellent view for miles over the surrounding countryside, affording ample time for the alarm to be sounded by the sentry at the initial appearance of a possibly hostile force. The peasants, who by now depended on their lord for their livelihood, and who would have to help defend the walls, would rush into the cover of the bailey with their cattle, swine and families. They could expect no mercy from any invader, and little from the troops of their lord's overlord, or neighbor, whoever had ordered the attack. Some of these castles were in view of each other, providing mutual support, and many were sited strategically to defend ports and estuaries, the entry into valleys, passes through hill features and ethnic boundaries. A map of William I's castles after his occupation of England shows a tight cluster all along the border with Wales and a concentration along the hilly "spine" of central England. This explains why so many of these castles, originally fairly simple, were strengthened, rebuilt, enlarged, or modernized over the centuries on their well-chosen sites. Old, forgotten boundaries in France and Germany can be traced by marking the profusion of castles built along them. The castles on major trade routes and navigable rivers were set there to enforce the payment of tolls and duties, and those ostensibly defending towns collected a good steady income by taxing the inhabitants, including the merchants who lived there, or those who came to the markets, which were jealously licensed. The protection thus afforded might often be considered a worthwhile expense.

It is useful here to point out that the castle's role was by no means purely defensive, as popular opinion today would have it. It was a symbol of the naked aggression and avarice that permeated the cultures of those times. The castle, while providing a secure residence for its owner, was also a firm base from which to dominate the surrounding countryside. It is thought that a troop of mounted men-at-arms could cover an operational radius of some 20 miles (32 km) from their base in a day, returning to the safety of the castle before nightfall. A peasant in arrears for his rent, his tithe to the priest, or the labor he owed his master, would very soon have his faults painfully pointed out to him by a burly sergeant. A castle could also function as the secure assembly point and springboard for an incursion into enemy territory, or a link in the logistical chain of an advancing allied force. The purely administrative function of a castle will be examined later.

As we have seen, there were traces of stone edifices across Europe before the popularity of the motte-and-bailey, and accounts of "strong stone houses" appear in eleventh-century literature. Carolingian forts, or halls, were converted into stone castles in Germany and France. It was, however, in these early stages of the feudal system that the proliferation of castles occurred. Often a ring-work defense was improved by building a motte within it (known as a *Kernmotte* in German-speaking lands, while *Herrenburg* was the term often used for a motte-and-bailey type residence).

The motte-and-bailey remained an extremely useful and economic form of castle for many years. However, it had two major disadvantages. Its vulnerability to fire was an obvious reason for seeking improvements,

Below: The stone keep, or donjon, would become the trademark of the Norman castle. The keep was the residence of the lord, the place of last retreat in a siege and the administrative hub of the estate (called a manor). Square or rectangular in plan, the keep rose several stories high, with crenellated battlements. Rectangular towers at each corner provided flanking fire along the faces of the walls. Their height made them good watchtowers and sites for warning beacons. The bases of the walls were widely splayed, so that missiles hurled from the battlements would bounce toward besiegers, and to make sapping and mining more difficult.

Opposite: One of the most impressive Norman stone keeps is at Rochester, England, guarding the route to London from the south. Replacing an earlier motte-and-bailey castle, Gundulf, Norman bishop of Rochester, built the walls that encircle the keep for William II (Rufus). Gundulf also supervised the building of the Conqueror's White Tower in London. In 1127 King Henry I empowered the archbishops of Canterbury to build a fortification within the castle, and hold it forever. This is undoubtedly the mighty donjon we see today.

and although large and luxurious towers did exist, most must have been rather cramped and uncomfortable. Once the urgency of the need for security had gone, the substitution of stone for wood could be effected. Stone construction was much more expensive than local wood, of course, especially if the quarry was some distance away, and it required the services of skilled workers, besides taking much longer. However, the remains of "shell keeps," as they are called, are still seen, mainly in England, less often on the Continent. The shell was a circular stone wall built around the perimeter of the motte, with possibly a stone gateway enclosing the stairs to the summit. A major problem was that the motte, if it was artificial, could be unstable and incapable of bearing too great a weight, thus limiting the size of any structure. The interior of the shell was divided into roofed-over living quarters built against the outside wall. A fine example of this type of keep can be seen at Restormal, in Cornwall, England. A shell keep at Gisors, a town built on a promontory of Normandy projecting into the Ile de France, was built on the original motte (first fortified in 1097) by the son of William the Conqueror, Henry I of England, Duke of Normandy. Of particular interest here is the fact that a very tall octagonal stone keep was later built inside the shell, probably by Henry's grandson, Henry II. A massive wall also surrounds the base of the motte, and it is probable, deduced from the huge weights involved, that the motte must have originally been a natural hill. Other examples of the addition of stonework to earlier castles are mottes on which the wooden tower had disappeared, and a wall (later to be called a curtain wall) had replaced the wooden palisade behind the ditch. In this case, it was probably not considered worth the effort of hauling large blocks of stone to the top of a step mound.

William I, King of England, the epitome of a Norman ruler, was a trendsetter in the long history of castle building. In addition to the need for security, he introduced another factor: status. A ruler who was secure in his sovereignty, and who had the resources of a kingdom to call upon, did not hold court in a wooden structure perched on a hillock. This might be in order for a knight who lived in some remote area on a smallish estate, but King William needed to impress and dominate his nobles, as well as the few Saxon lords who had survived. One means was to build very impressive, and extremely secure, stone castles, called keeps, an example followed by many nobles. It is as if William were saying, "Look at me! I, who was William the bastard, am now King William the Conquerer!" These massive keeps are the hallmarks of Norman-dominated lands. Before describing them, it is useful to know that keep is a relatively modern word, not used in the Middle Ages and confined to the English language. William would have said "donjon," as would his French-speaking contemporaries. In German-speaking lands, the term for a tall fortified tower is *Bergfried*, but it did not have the same importance as the tower-keep in France, England, Italy and Sicily, being more of a watchtower than a lordly residence. At this time, great lords preferred to build castles reminiscent of Carolingian palaces. The castle built by the Margrave of Thuringia around 1200, the Wartburg in Eisenach, is a good example, and Martin Luther must have appreciated the feeling of security this afforded him centuries later.

Unfortunately, the meaning of *donjon* in English has been corrupted into "dungeon," which has caused the main function of a castle to be confused in modern minds with that of a prison. This is certainly not the

Above: Chepstow Castle, in Gwent, Wales, built on a narrow spur of rock near the River Wye, was one of the first stone castles in Britain. Here, William FitzOsbern, Earl of Hertford, was entrusted by the Conqueror to guard the English border against the unconquered Welsh. A two-storied keep, finished in 1071, received another story in the thirteenth century. Later, the earl of Pembroke added a thick curtain wall and constructed the western bailey with a barbican. The huge D-end tower (c. 1270–1300), with its spur bases, is especially noteworthy as a significant advance in strengthening the defenses.

case. In the Middle Ages, prisons did not exist. A noble prisoner might be held securely in a castle until his ransom was paid, like Richard the Lionheart in Austria, or the Black Prince's prisoner, the king of France, after the battle of Poitiers (1356). Customs and laws varied greatly from country to country, and from time to time, but a common prisoner might well have been held in the cellars of a castle only until his lord could find time to deal with him. Once found guilty, or not even then, his fate would not be imprisonment for a period of months or years. A poacher would probably have a hand cut off, if he were not hanged, or a thief be branded. Others suspected of crimes could be faced with one of the several harrowing trials by ordeal. To be burnt at the stake, particularly for heresy, was not an uncommon end. Instruments of torture in the vaults of many castles did not prove that the owner was a greater sadist than others: often, a confession was not considered valid unless made

under torture, or "duress." The Inquisition, and the antiwitch mania that swept Europe later revived the popularity of torture in many lands, but that was toward the end of the Middle Ages and afterward. There were certainly windowless, airless cellars in the base of many towers, with access only through a hatch in the roof. Some of these were also the receptors for the castle's sewage and had to be cleaned out occasionally. It may be that a prisoner was thrown into one of these and then forgotten, hence the name *oubliette*, but this was probably the exception rather than the rule, since it was unnecessary in an age when life was held so cheaply. Perhaps we owe this persistent myth to romantic novelists and the authors of guidebooks. Only when castles were no longer needed were many turned into prisons. Having been designed to keep people out, they could easily serve to keep people in. The Bastille in Paris is a good example of this, after its use as a residence was obviated.

However, to avoid confusion, we shall continue to use the word "keep" as it has been defined here. There were two kinds of rectangular keep in the twelfth century, now known as hall-keeps and tower-keeps. The former were squat and rectangular, two stories high, rather like blockhouses. The better-known tower-keeps were square, rising to four stories. A prime example of an early keep was that built by William I at Colchester, on Roman foundations, but the most famous keep of all was what we now call the White Tower in the Tower of London. This was begun in about 1070, in an angle of the old Roman town walls, with a bailey running down to the Thames. As we have seen, it was painted white, hence its name, which still survives. The builder was William's friend and retainer Gundulf, who was later to become Bishop of Rochester, where he built a stunning cathedral and, of course, an exemplary tower-keep. The Norman conquerors often built cathedrals next to their major castles. Canterbury Cathedral, the oldest in England, dating back to 597, was burnt to the ground a year after the invasion, and William's Norman Archbishop (Lanfranc) built a magnificent Norman cathedral on the ruins; a Norman tower-keep nearby soon followed (about 1080) to complement it. In Durham, the bishop, who would have been called a prince-bishop in Germany, since he was the secular ruler of the Marches between

Below: The White Tower. A famous London landmark, this Norman rectangular keep was built on the site of William the Conqueror's original earthwork enclosure, begun in 1066 in the southeastern corner of the old Roman walls of the city. In 1078 William began construction of this stone donjon, one of the first and largest in Britain; his son, William II (Rufus) completed it late in the 1190s.

Richmond Castle
North Yorkshire, England

Left: This window in the keep shows how immensely thick the walls were. It may once have been an arrow loop, enlarged in a more peaceable age. ***Below, left:*** A door to the keep: the main entrance was on the second floor, opening off the curtain-wall walkway.

Richmond Castle's 100-foot (31.0m) stone keep (shown below, at the center of the photograph), was built during the second half of the twelfth century above an original gatehouse dating from 1090. This structure would have been blocked when the keep was built, but was opened up again much later. The keep's entrance is on the second floor, opening off the wall-walk of the curtain; straight staircases lead between floors inside the keep and from the keep's interior onto the crenellated battlements. Each corner of the keep has its own two-story square-shaped turrets.

The castle is triangular in plan, with the keep at the apex, and is bounded by a curtain wall that is 10 feet (3.0m) thick, the base of which is built along the edge of a cliff on the banks of the River Swale. Jutting out from the curtain, next to Scolland's Hall, is the quaintly named "Gold Hole Tower," which houses the eleventh-century latrines.

Below: A view looking north from the opposite bank of the River Swale. The steep cliff, topped by a stout curtain wall, made Richmond a formidable obstacle. The keep is in the center, and the Great Hall is to the right.

Inside a Norman Keep

A typical Norman keep, or donjon, was built of stone to a height of up to 90 feet (27m). The walls, usually 12 to 15 feet (4 to 5m) thick, were battered (splayed) at the base for added protection against sapping or mining and to deflect missiles hurled from above. Buttresses were some-

times added to reinforce the walls. Towers at each corner often had turrets to provide extra height for improved visibility over the surrounding area. The keep housed the lord and his family, provided refuge during sieges, and was the administrative headquarters of the castle.

Turret: extra firing positions; extra height as watchtower; access to roof covered

Crenellated battlements

Arrow loops

Great hall, two stories high

Storage space

Batter: to deflect missiles dropped from above and to hinder sapping

Entrance turret, with two portcullises and drawbridge to forebuilding

Bailey: area between keep and outer walls

Firing positions, crenellated

Towers at each corner with spiral staircases to all floors

Solar, or private apartment for lord and family

Crenellated battlements covering ramp and entrance turret

Windows with window alcove set in wall

Forebuilding, often housing a chapel

Living space, chambers, and latrines set into walls

Main entrance to forebuilding

Wide gap between turret and main entrance in forebuilding, crossed by drawbridge (not shown in this illustration)

England and Scotland, also positioned his Norman castle and cathedral side-by-side. It was implied that the conquered people were under Norman rule, body and soul.

Even without the leadership of their duke, the Normans took their military skills, originally as emigrants, to Italy and Sicily, remaining there as rulers. The Hautville brothers arrived in Apulia in southern Italy in 1035. Many Norman knights were there already, employed as mercenaries. Fighting, first against the Muslims on the side of a Byzantine army, and later in revolt against them, resulted in the establishment of a Norman kingdom there. The Norman castles in Melfi, Squillace and San Marco Argentano in Calabria are evidence of their success in founding what have been described by Professor R.C.H. Davis of Birmingham University as "rich, populous, strategically important territories, [which] fostered a remarkable civilization blending Latin, Greek and Arabic elements—a sort of intellectual clearing house between East and West." As far as their castle architecture is concerned, this was a precursor of the Crusades.

A brief description here of a typical keep will give some idea of the challenge facing an attacker. The walls were constructed of whatever stone was available, and could be 90 feet (27m) high and 12 to 15 feet (4–5m) thick. The walls were normally splayed out at their bases, or battered, providing extra thickness and added protection against sapping and mining. A missile dropped from the battlements would bounce off this batter, and could damage an attacker where it hurt most. The walls could be strengthened with buttresses, and there was normally a tower at each corner, which could enclose a spiral staircase. These towers were often furnished with turrets some 12 feet (3.6m) high, to provide a view over a greater distance. The walls were castellated, and the building consisted of three

or four stories, with timber flooring. The entrance was normally on the first or second floor, rather than the ground floor, and was gained by stairs, exposed to the defenders, rising to a forebuilding. This was a substantial edifice built onto the main structure, two or three stories high, and defended by a stout gate and portcullis, over a drawbridge covered by loopholes set in the main castle walls. Here an attacker who had penetrated so far found himself in a large antechamber, where he would have to force a massive gate set at right-angles in order to gain entrance.

Above: The sophisticated design of this Chepstow Castle window, next to a Gothic doorway, reveals that it was part of the late thirteenth-century major rebuilding, when the lower bailey was constructed and elaborate domestic accommodation added to the original eleventh-century stone castle.

Below: Mural tower detail at one of Ireland's great Norman castles, Trim, County Meath, which stands on the banks of the River Boyne, enclosing some 3 acres (1.2 hectares). It is thought that the stone castle dates from the late twelfth century and was built on the site of an earlier timber fortress, although there was no motte. The castle was eventually surrendered to Cromwellian forces in 1650.

The basement would be used for storage, while the lord's main accommodation, the great hall, was on the first or second floor. This would normally be partitioned into the main living space and private chambers—retiring rooms—for the lord and his family. These quarters would include such creature comforts as large fireplaces and latrines, *garderobes*. A good internal well, with access from each story, was an absolute necessity. The area of the ground plan could vary tremendously, but the dimensions of the White Tower are not atypical, 118 feet by 107 feet (35.9 x 32.6m), and 90 feet (27.4m) high. A fine rectangular keep is still to be seen at Falaise in Normandy, built by William's son Henry. Loches, in Touraine, has exceptional semicircular buttresses. There is also a fine Norman keep in Sicily, at Adrano.

The vulnerable points of these keeps were the square corners of the towers, which could be mined more easily than the walls. This was shown when a later king of England, John, the much-hated younger brother of Richard the Lionheart, besieged Rochester castle in 1215. Gundulf's bailey walls, built on Roman foundations, were soon breached, and five massive stone-throwing engines set up, which pounded the keep day and night to no avail. John, who was personally in command, then decided to mine. He ordered "as many picks as you are able" to be manufactured in nearby Canterbury, and commissioned Hubert de Burgh, his justiciar (a kind of regent) to "Send to us with all speed by day forty of the fattest pigs of the sort least good for eating to bring fire beneath the tower." The mine was dug and the shoring

destroyed when the pigs were consumed by the conflagration. Their fat fueled the flames, and the tower was breached. Castle builders had learned a lesson, and repairs were made using a circular tower, which was much less vulnerable. This is probably why other circular or octagonal keeps were built, some of them aesthetically beautiful.

One of the earliest round keeps can be found in Frétval in the Loire Valley; it is thought to date from the late eleventh century. This is a simple cylinder, 100 feet (30.5m) high, with a diameter of 50 feet (15.3m). An interesting contrast of styles is seen at Falaise, where next to Henry I's rectangular keep mentioned above, Philip Augustus of France built a large, round, machicolated tower. A very good example of a round keep in Britain is at Pembroke, in Wales. This great round tower (built c. 1200–10) rises from a splayed plinth to some 80 feet (24.4m) high, and is 53 feet (16.2m)

in diameter. The walls are some 16 feet (4.9m) thick, and it is capped by a stone dome 4 feet (1.2m) thick. This was the birthplace of Henry Tudor, later Henry VII of England. Space prevents the description of many other fine round tower-keeps, which at this time were being built mainly in France and England. However, one octagonal English tower keep should be mentioned. This is at Orford, in Suffolk, built between 1166 and 1172. It is unique in having a polygonal plan, with three rectangular towers evenly spaced around the walls. However, here we leave the era of the early castles and move on to the next stage in our journey through time: the developments in England and France that led to the important struggles between Angevins and Capetians, the cause of the Hundred Years' War between them, and the Crusades, probably the most significant event in the development of castles since the feudal system began to evolve.

Above: This picture shows the keep of Trim castle, behind its curtain wall, and mural towers. The square keep is almost 76 feet (23.2m) tall; a square turret was placed centrally on each of the walls (one of which is now missing). The 11-foot-thick walls (3.4m) are battered at the base. The two lower stories were built in 1200, while the final stages were completed around 1220.

The Tower of London
London, England

The Tower of London, with its Norman keep and towering battlements, is one of the world's most famous historic monuments. William the Conqueror built his first fortress here in 1066 in the Roman city walls, alongside the River Thames. The great keep (White Tower), finished later, is 90 feet (27.5m) tall and is the most complete eleventh-century royal residence in Europe. King Henry III strengthened the defenses with two towers incorporated in a riverside curtain wall and built a massive western wall that was reinforced later with three great D-shaped towers. His son, Edward I, surrounded the castle with an outer curtain wall (c. 1300) and a moat overlooked by two massive bastions.

Left: The crenellated battlements on this tower probably owe their decorative faux machicolations to a Victorian restorer's enthusiasm.

Right: One of the four corner turrets of the Norman keep.

Below, left: These simple but effective arrow loops are in Edward I's outer curtain wall.

Below, right: Traitor's Gate, so called because prisoners brought here for execution entered from the River Thames through this water gate.

CRUSADER CASTLES AND THEIR LEGACY

Although most authorities state that the Crusades had a significant influence on medieval castle design, many do not explain exactly how and when, or indeed, which Crusade was involved. In addressing these questions concisely, there is a danger of oversimplification, since not only did the convoluted political and religious affairs of medieval Europe affect the outcome significantly, so also did the complicated internal dynastic and ethnic struggles of the Muslim world.

In this chapter, we shall consider the effect on castles engendered by the major Crusades of the Latin Christian world. The most influential were those that originated with the call made by Pope Urban II, who proclaimed what is known as the First Crusade in 1095. The aim was mainly to reconquer and occupy the "Holy Land" of Christ's birth, which had been wrested from the Byzantine Empire by what we shall call the Muslims. (Medieval writers referred to them collectively as Saracens [including Arabs and Seljuk Turks], a term derived from the name of a Bedouin tribe.) A less well-known crusade was the reconquest of the Iberian Peninsula (Spain and Portugal) from the Berber (North-African Arab) Muslims who had invaded through Gibraltar in 711 and penetrated as far as Poitiers when their advance was halted in 732, by Charles Martel, the grandfather of Charlemagne. Success was finally achieved in 1492 when Granada fell to the Christian forces. In reading of these epic struggles between Latin Christians and Islam, the fact that both sides called the other "Infidel" can cause confusion. Another rather different Crusade was the conquest and occupation of Slavic lands by the Order of Teutonic Knights, an ethnic German monastic order founded in the

Holy Land in 1198. All these Crusades, to a greater or lesser extent, involved military experts from many countries and cultures who could share common experiences in siege warfare and cross-fertilize new ideas about building and defending castles.

THE HOLY LAND

In considering those Crusades that occupy such an important niche in our concept of the Middle Ages, and which, some authors believe, had a seminal effect upon the evolution of European castles derived from Palestine and Syria, we find two opposing overall views. Geoffrey Chaucer, the great fourteenth-century English poet, did not mince words when he described certain stereotypical characters of his time, but he obviously had a profound respect for the crusading knight, "a true, a perfect gentleknight," and, by implication, for the Crusades, as seen in the *General Prologue to the Canterbury Tales*.

A leading modern historian of the Crusades held a very different view. Sir Steven Runciman, in his *History of the Crusades*, described the Crusaders as the last wave of the barbarian invaders who had destroyed the Roman Empire. They accomplished this by destroying the true center of medieval civilization and the last bastion of antiquity, Constantinople and the Byzantine Empire. Runciman's hypercritical view is shared by many scholars today: "High ideals were besmirched by cruelty and greed, enterprise and endurance by a blind and narrow self righteousness: and the Holy war itself was nothing more than a long act of intolerance in the name of God, which is a sin against the Holy Ghost." [!]

What is the true picture? The answer probably lies in the attitudes of the writers. Of course, Chaucer was well aware of the barbarity of warfare in his own time.

Previous pages: La Calahorra in Granada, Spain, was built after the Moors were finally expelled from Spain (in 1492). The castle was completed in 1512 as a residence for the marquis of Zenete, named for a Moorish village in the estate he had been granted on the remote northern slopes of the Sierra Nevada. The rectangular building is two stories high and has large circular towers, each crowned with a dome, at each corner. La Calahorra is a unique compromise between an artillery fort and a sumptuous palace. The stark exterior belies a beautiful and elegant interior.

The Krak des Chevaliers

Krak des Chevaliers (Castle of the Knights) was the major stronghold of the Hospitallers, the order of military monks, who, together with the Templars, were the main "regular" forces of the Crusaders. The best-known of the many Crusader castles, Krak des Chevaliers is justifiably world-renowned. In 1144 Count Raymond II of Tripoli granted the Hospitallers a huge estate, and they concentrated their extensive resources on defending and dominating their new rich, fertile lands. The castle was built by the lord of Oultrejourdain (present-day Jordan).

The Hospitallers established their fortress, "the finest and most elaborately fortified in the Crusader Levant" (Hugh Kennedy, *Crusader Castles*), on the site of an earlier castle owned by the emir of Homs, on a steep spur of the Syrian hills. After losing their land and castles in the south in 1187, the Hospitallers concentrated their resources on defending the eastern frontiers of the state of Tripoli, and administering their own large holdings there.

The castle fulfilled its purpose, sheltering the inhabitants of the Hospitallers' lands in Tripoli when they were ravaged by Saladin in 1180, and again in 1188. As an experienced soldier, Saladin realized that it was useless to besiege such a strong and well-manned fortress.

In the first half of the thirteenth century, Krak des Chevaliers was the only inland Crusader castle to remain continuously in Christian possession. During this period, the 2,000-strong garrison not only profited from the produce of its own lands, but the mounted knights exacted tribute from the Muslims of Homs, Hama and neighboring districts. A decline began in 1250; in 1271 the Mamluke Sultan Baybars breached the castle's outer walls, and surrender terms were negotiated.

Detail views of this castle are shown on the previous pages and above, with the full castle featured at right. On page 64, Spain's Castillo de Albuquerque, which, like many Spanish castles, reflects the influence of the Crusader castles.

The horrors that Sir Steven denounced were commonplace all over Europe and the Middle East. As a twentieth-century observer, he weighed medieval ethics against his own modern and idealistic views including those of contemporary Christianity. Chaucer credits his knight with the qualities of chivalry—"truth, honor, generousness and courtesy"—a quasi-religious code of behavior to be touched upon later. It is sufficient to say here that chivalry had little to do with actual warfare, except for the treatment of prisoners who could pay ransom, or the conduct of the mock wars involved in tournaments and jousting, which lie outside the scope of this book. It did, however, have an effect upon the motives of some Crusaders and the bishops and priests who exhorted and accompanied them. Their concept of Christianity was heavily weighted by superstition and dread of eternal punishment (often illustrated in grisly detail in ecclesiastical artwork) for "sins" that were specified by the Church. Anyone who took part in a Crusade was granted absolution from his sins: for example, the four knights who murdered Thomas Becket, the Archbishop of Canterbury, in 1170.

What has all this to do with castles? We are exploring the motives of the Crusaders, which led them to embark on a dangerous and expensive enterprise involving attacks upon fortified strongholds, their capture and their construction. Many powerful rulers went on the First Crusade, and indeed, on several of the later ones. Kings, dukes and counts are all recorded, and most acquitted themselves well, earning the stature and respect accorded in Europe to valor, military prowess and devotion. For our purpose, we shall divide the Crusaders into two main categories: those who came to the Holy Land, did their duty and returned home; and those who stayed. The former were the great princes who ruled vast lands at home, which they had to protect from the very many who would take full advantage of their absence. Meanwhile, they had acquired enviable reputations for boldness and valor. Robert, Duke of Normandy, eldest son of the Conqueror, pawned his duchy to his younger brother, King William II (Rufus) of England, to raise the funds needed to go on Crusade, which eventually lost him his inheritance.

In the second category are those Crusaders who stayed on in the Holy Land. One very significant result of the feudal system's becoming hereditary (i.e., that the title and lands were inherited by the eldest son—called primogeniture), was that the younger sons, reared and trained as aristocratic warriors, usually in some great lord's castle, had no lands of their own, and, most importantly, no income. Apart from entering the Church, no other method of earning a living was open to them. Many could not even afford the considerable sum required to buy a good warhorse and decent

Below: The Krak des Chevaliers has good access to the Dead Sea, and was bordered on all three sides by steep slopes. Only on the southern apex did it border the main plateau of Moab, where a ditch cut into the rocks augmented the defenses. It was separated from the associated town on its northern side by a 100-foot deep (30m) ditch, now almost filled in. The detail shown below illustrates the thickness of the castle walls, while the photograph on page 57 shows the battered outer walls.

armor. Their only method of earning a living was to enlist as retainers in the service of a lord who would pay them and provide them with a mount and accouterments. One of the senior leaders of the First Crusade, Raymond of St. Giles, Count of Toulouse and Marquis of Provence, had 10,000 men in his train, including 1,000 knights and mounted men-at-arms. The Crusades offered these landless men the chance to acquire foreign estates and remain as lords over them, building castles and squeezing an income from an alien peasantry. Their aim was to convert the conquered lands into a replica of their homelands, dominated by their castles and inhabited by their families and retainers. Their vassals would owe them allegiance and dues, and they could exact tolls and taxes from the trade routes and towns in their possession, in return for protection. The disadvantage was that they lived under constant threat from their own serfs, and from sudden or sustained attacks by the Saracens from whom they had seized the territory. Many Muslims were just as committed to a holy war as were the Christian Crusaders, and for many of the same reasons. No wonder that the Holy Land became known as the land of Crusader and Saracen castles.

Once the Crusaders had arrived in Constantinople in 1097, they promised the Byzantine emperor homage and recognition of his imperial overlordship in all reconquered lands, in return for supplies and support in their difficult and dangerous journey across Anatolia. Like so many Middle-Age vows and promises, this was soon forgotten when they reached the Holy Land. After tremendous hardships, they arrived at the northernmost city, Antioch, in 1097, and captured it after a long and brutal siege. Here the Crusaders started to learn their first hard-earned lessons, and

were initiated into war against an Oriental enemy ensconced in a strongly defended fortified town. At this stage, one of their ablest leaders, the Norman Bohemund of Taranto, the disinherited son of the Norman ruler of southern Italy and Sicily, set himself up as prince of one of the largest Crusader states, the Principality of Antioch. Thereafter, Bohemund and his knights were busy consolidating and defending their newly won estates (often from each other). Raymond of Toulouse, younger son of the Crusaders' leader Godfrey of Lorraine, hoped to gain this great prize for himself, but had to be content with the County of Tripoli. Baldwin, Godfrey's younger brother, established himself as Count of Edessa, on the Euphrates River in Syria, but he was with his brother when Jerusalem fell to the Crusaders in 1099, when many thousands of Arab and Jewish inhabitants were slaughtered. He became king of Jerusalem on his brother's death. Bohemund's nephew, Tancred, became prince of Galilee.

The Crusader conquests and establishment of feudal states soon turned the coastal plain of the Levant into a huge melting pot of cultures, including experience and skills in all aspects of warfare. The expression "lingua franca" (French tongue) was coined here, although this common language included contributions from Spanish, Greek, Arabic, Italian and Turkish in addition to the language of the Franks. Knights from northern France, Anjou, Poitu and Normandy traditionally built stone donjons, as we have seen. Others came from Lotharingia, the land of Godfrey and Baldwin, on either side of the modern French-Belgian border. Historically, they had built enclosure castles of varying size on ridges and hilltops. Some did have donjons but, apparently, they were not as important as in the Norman and northern

French tradition. A major castle near Liège, which belonged to a bishop, enclosed an area of some 12 acres (5 hectares) within its curtain wall, which had square towers along the perimeter. It had no donjon, but there was a central strong point. A neighboring bishop's castle, much smaller and more compact, had quite a large donjon, but it protruded from the curtain wall and was not a major element in the overall defense. In Champagne, fortified sites consisted mainly of mottes in the low-lying areas, and enclosure castles, where possible, on spurs and ridges. Provence also had mottes in the lowlands, as well as spur and ridge enclosures.

Although Normans from southern Italy and Sicily were the principal settlers in Antioch, there is little evidence of great stone towers here, even though their situation—alien conquerors in a hostile land—

was similar. In fact, as seen later, many Christian Armenians who lived there welcomed the Crusaders and were themselves master castle builders. It would seem, however, that the Crusaders originally built castles reflecting the norm in their homelands, as could be expected. They had also seen, and in many cases besieged and captured, the sophisticated, massive defenses built over the years by the Byzantines and manned by Turks. Clearly, they eventually learned to build more advanced castles from the Byzantines, Muslims and Armenians. The Prussian military historian Karl von Clausewitz tells us in his masterful *On War* (1833, Bk II, Ch VI): "If any means is once found efficacious in War, it is repeated; one nation copies another, the thing becomes the fashion, and in this manner it comes into use, supported by experience, and takes

Below: The interactive effect of the Crusades on castle design is seen here in the town of Collioure, in the Catalan area of France. Not only did Catalonia share a language with its kinsmen in Spain, but the church and fortifications in this bay resemble those of Spain, and, for that matter, of the twelfth-century Holy Land.

its place in theory." This *weisheit* (wisdom) is particularly relevant to the evolution of castles, and to siege warfare in general.

The massive, antique defenses of Constantinople must have amazed the first Crusaders, but their scope was impossible to replicate. The invaders soon found that these Byzantine fortifications, now manned by Muslims, presented far greater difficulties than expected. Their first two attempts to take such fortresses were not encouraging: Nicaea and Antioch were defended by single high curtain walls supported by numerous boldly projecting square and polygonal towers, in which the defenders could live and keep close watch over the enemy. Neither of these castles could be taken by direct assault.

Another form of defensive building the Crusaders saw in their travels across Anatolia was the citadel, perched high on a crag, ridge, or steep hill, which provided a refuge for local inhabitants when attack threatened. One of these can still be seen at Ankara, where a noticeable feature is the number of massive interval towers, of various ground plans, that jut out aggressively from the wall. This example has two baileys, but no donjon. The Byzantines had built a number of smaller, but well-fortified, castles in northern Syria in the last half of the eleventh century, which the Crusaders occupied after capturing them from the Muslims. These could have served as models for the many small perimeter castles built in western Europe in the face of the Ottoman Turks' relentless advance.

Contrary to popular belief, there is evidence that the Crusaders found many of the later Byzantine fortifications inadequate and improved them along Western lines, using stone blocks to replace rubble masonry and replacing or adding more substantial towers. It is difficult to know, a

millennium afterward, who was copying whom when comparing the details of the castle at Korikos in Cilicia, one of the more advanced Byzantine castles, with some of those the Crusaders built later. Some authorities consider that this served as the prototype of the castles that later dominated European design; others are not so sure. A Byzantine admiral built Korikos early in the twelfth century with inner and outer lines of walls, the inner one being much taller, dominating the outer, as in the defenses of Constantinople. The inner walls have numerous projecting flanking towers, and the construction is of large stone blocks, probably reused from an antique fortress. The rectangular castle was protected by the sea on two sides, and by marshes on the third, while a ditch cut into the rock protected the fourth. It could almost be identified as the first concentric castle. The Armenians built castles for the occupation of their noble families, in line with Western practice, producing a form that was not only copied widely by the Crusaders, but included features that were models for many castles built in the West in the thirteenth century. Perched on crags and outcrops, their curtain walls closely followed the edges of precipitous cliffs and were supported by large, boldly projecting circular flanking towers armed with arrow slits. Such round towers, although they required more skillful construction, had four great advantages: they were much stronger than a square tower and could withstand the pounding of the great rocks flung from a trebuchet, or a battering ram, much longer; lacking corners (the weakest point of a rectangle), they were resistant to mining; they deflected the impact of missiles; and had fewer "blind spots" that protected attackers from the view of defending archers and slingers.

Surprisingly, there is little evidence to show that the Turks had developed an effective castle design of their own. They appeared to occupy, and repair where necessary, castles they had captured from the Byzantines or the Crusaders. There is ample evidence that they enlarged or improved these, but little trace remains of "typical" Turkish castles. Those that could have been Muslim-built are rather similar to Roman predecessors—rectangular, with small round or square towers at the corners. The Arab caliphates, too, were not known as great castle builders (except in Spain), but the defenses of Cairo deserve special mention. These are attributed to the great Saladin (a Kurd), who finally took Jerusalem from the Crusaders, and whose military prowess persuaded another great warrior, Richard the Lionheart, that the time had come to make peace, gain a guarantee of safe passage to Jerusalem for pilgrims and return to France to secure his lands there.

The exceptional role played by the three major orders of military monks—the Templars, Hospitallers and Teutonic Order—was instrumental in enabling the Crusaders to hold on in the Holy Land as long as they did. The Templars were so named because of their initial quarters in the "Temple of Solomon" in Jerusalem (built, in fact, by Herod the Great on the site of Solomon's Temple). The Hospitallers (Knights of St. John), were originally founded to care for pilgrims and the sick, and the Teutonic Knights were ethnic Germans. These three orders became the Crusaders' only dependable regular army. They were not individually motivated by personal gain, and because of very considerable financial support from Europe, were able to build castles that were beyond the means of many nobles. The Templars in particular, responsible only to the pope, became so wealthy and influential (they were bankers to many of the rulers) that they attracted

Below: The magnificent palace of the Grand Master of the Hospitallers in Rhodes, the Order's headquarters from 1309 until 1552, when the Ottoman Turks finally captured the island. The fortress was built after the destructive earthquake of 1481 and stands within the massive walls of the inner defenses, together with a beautiful hospital, behind the Gate of Amboise.

Below: Musandam Al Khasab, Oman. Although its interior was inhabited by Bedouin nomads, the coast of Oman, in southeast Arabia, was quite fertile. The Arabs here were great seafarers and traders, especially with the lands of the Indus delta. They also turned their hands to piracy, since a major trade route to Akab passed their doorstep on the Straits of Hormuz. Their own fort, shown below, would give them protection from seaborne robbers and a safe base.

the jealousy of the king of France, Philip IV, who suppressed them in 1313, with the co-operation of his minion, Pope Clement V, with unbelievable cruelty. Their possessions in the Levant were transferred to the Hospitallers, who had, generally speaking, the pragmatic outlook on war of professionals. They used their magnificent castles for shelter and defense when they perceived that an outright frontal assault against overwhelmingly superior forces had little or no hope of success. Even Saladin acknowledged their superiority, and they received special treatment when captured. Their castles were much larger than the norm, since they were also monasteries, mandated to accommodate many knights at need.

Two of the main Hospitaller castles deserve mention as representatives of masterful castle design. Krak (or Crac) des Chevaliers is probably the world's most famous castle. The Hospitallers built it in the twelfth and thirteenth centuries on the

original site of a Kurdish garrison. Throughout its existence as a Crusader stronghold it survived, and deterred, many fierce attacks, and served as the springboard for mighty shows of force to persuade various Saracen magnates to pay the tributes exacted from them. The Templars often sent strong contingents in support, and the stronghold exemplified the essence of a castle's raison d'etre: to dominate and menace a wide area and to provide an impregnable retreat when attacked by a superior force. At the height of its activity, it could house 2,000, and its fall, in 1271, was due mainly to lack of funds. The garrison had shrunk to some 300, a hopelessly inadequate number to man the extensive walls, especially against the determined attack of a rising Mamluke potentate called Baybars, who added a square tower to the center of the southern outer wall.

Built in a mountainous district, Krak des Chevaliers had no towering donjon to provide a prime target for a devastating trebuchet, but there were two concentric curtain walls, enclosing an inner and outer bailey. The north end is on the edge of a precipitous, clifflike hillside, which is where a postern gate is located. Both of the southern bailey walls, facing the likeliest direction of attack, are furnished with three powerful towers. The inner wall is high above the outer, and its battlements therefore dominate both the inner and outer baileys. The main gate is in the eastern side of the outer wall, toward the north: thus it could be approached from the south only by forcing an outer doorway; then navigating up a long, narrow, twisting tunnel, also furnished with gates; and commanded by machicolations from which missiles and Greek fire could be poured. This passage-

Above: Taba, Gulf of Aqaba. This castle on an island off the Egyptian Sinai coast in the Gulf of Aqaba, just south of the Israeli port of Eilat, is something of a conundrum. It was originally thought to be a Crusader fort, built by Baldwin I in 1115, when he crossed the Negev Desert to build the great castle of Montreal. Taba was thought to be an outpost of the castle at Montreal, designed to strengthen Crusader control of the gulf. However, later studies suggest that it was a Muslim stronghold, designed to curb the Crusaders' attempts to extort tolls from their traders. Perhaps both views are correct, since castles often changed hands.

Above: Krak de Montreal was an early castle built in 1115 by Baldwin I. His aim was to control the rich caravan routes from Damascus to Egypt and the Muslim Holy Places. Having selected an isolated conical hill on the plateau of Edom (now Shawbak, Jordan), he built a strong castle on top, described in a contemporary account as "a most excellent fortress, surrounded by triple walls." After the castle fell to the Muslims in 1188, the Crusader building was incorporated into a Mamluke fort, but traces of a curtain wall and two chapels can still be seen.

way, having folded back upon itself, terminates in a massive gateway guarded by a portcullis and a very strong gate. The walls are strengthened by massive glacis—slopes that expose attackers to defensive fire. A contemporary report stated that the huge storage areas could accommodate several years' supplies, and the water storage capacity was such that there was never a shortage, even during the longest siege. Despite its semi-ruinous state, Krak retains the sort of beauty immanent in functional perfection and an air of menace still emanates from its forbidding walls.

What has been called a sister castle to Krak is Margat, some 37 miles (60 km) to the north. It stands on a steep, isolated hill overlooking the Mediterranean and dominating the surrounding countryside. Although not much smaller than Krak, it lacks its beauty, being constructed of hard black basalt rather than white limestone. It also differs from Krak in having a massive

circular donjon: the Hospitallers purchased the castle in 1186, and the square towers on the outer eastern wall probably date from the pre-Hospitaller era, before these forms went out of fashion. A castle-town, also encircled by a strong wall, is joined to the single southern curtain wall. Possibly this is where Edward I of England got his idea of a castle-town, since we know that many of his castles replicate features he saw on his Crusade. The other two sides (the castle is built on a triangular hill and follows its edge closely) are protected by double walls, built into the precipitous hillside. The inner walls tower over both the outer, and also over the inner bailey. The main gate (there is only one entrance) is approached from within the strongly defended castle-town, through the lower floor of a square gatehouse—machicolated and including a portcullis. A walkway between the curtain walls, making two right-angled turns, leads to a gatehouse in the inner walls. This in turn leads into a long, sloping passage, ending in another sharp turn before access to the citadel is achieved. The Hospitallers added four massive circular towers to the outer western walls, and to the southeast, where the approach is somewhat less steep, a large open cistern for rainwater (*berquilla*) was constructed to prevent tunneling. The castle is also remarkable for the two other massive rounded towers that the Hospitallers built. The smaller is at the northeast corner, while at the south is a huge rounded donjon 22 yards (20m) in diameter and 26 yards (24m) high. It is interesting to note that the inner chamber of this round tower is square, making the walls up to 11 yards (10m) thick, with vast storage vaults for enough food to last five years. However, in 1285, after a desperate defense against a greatly superior force, when several tunnels that were about to be opened into the citadel had been constructed, the commander accepted very favorable terms, and twenty-five of the senior knights in full armor led the garrison out. It is a poignant insight into the

decline of the Crusades that the Master of the Order wrote to Edward I of England in 1281 to say that although the castle was still adequately manned, he was in desperate need of funds to maintain it. By then, Edward had embarked on his hugely expensive program of castle building in Wales.

The jury is still out on the question of whether the Crusader and Muslim castles, which certainly were mutually influential, had very great influence on contemporary European castles, or vice versa. The verdict will probably be that the influence was reciprocal, since the exchange of expertise throughout two centuries must have had a tremendous effect upon all forms of warfare, and as we shall see, Europe was no stranger to armed conflict throughout this period. What did emerge clearly was the importance of tunneling in conducting a siege, and the devastating effect of the trebuchet, which brought a whole new power to siege artillery. Both factors had a notable effect upon castle design, which then remained largely unchanged until the advent of effective cannons.

Below: El Real de Manzanares near Madrid, Spain, which is famous as the land of castles. If the purpose of the late fifteenth-century builder, the first duke of El Infantado, was to impress, he certainly succeeded. On an outcrop of the rocky Guadarrame Mountains, it overlooks the Manzanares River, and one could imagine that it was built as a stout, rectangular, concentric castle to provide a strong defense. However, the architecture, combining late Gothic, Mudéjar and Renaissance styles to beautiful effect, is rather deceptive. Although furnished with arrow and handgun loops, and soaring crenellated turrets on the towers, it was really a sumptuous palace.

Above: Superlatives on the subject of Spanish castles abound, but the Alcázar of Segovia is truly exceptional. The favorite residence of Spanish royalty until the advent of the Habsburgs, its many beautiful buildings and architectural styles not only reflect the needs and tastes of successive monarchs, they also combine to form a breathtaking view of what must be the ultimate in castles. Of particular interest is the last of the medieval buildings, the massive keep, which is crowned with twelve turretlike bartizans. The Mudéjar style is evident throughout, both externally and in the magnificently restored interiors.

THE RECONQUEST OF SPAIN

We have seen that the Berbers invaded Spain in 711 and were halted in their advance on Western Europe at Poitiers in 732. Charlemagne continued to contain them, drove them southward, and established the Spanish March—a narrow strip of territory south of the mountainous border with France and north of the Ebro River, which formed the basis of the new Christian kingdoms of Navarre and Aragon. Space does not permit a detailed account of the reconquest that ensued until the Muslims were finally expelled in 1492, nor can we examine the dynastic struggles among both Muslims and Christians that continually broke out over the intervening six centuries. It was a slow, unsteady, advance, with the Christians sometimes forced to retreat from their new possessions, only to press forward again. The foundation of the northern Christian Kingdom of Leon and Castile gave further impetus to this advance. By 1100 King Ferdinand I was ensconced in Toledo, El Cid's widow ruled in Valencia and the kingdom of Portugal (at least the north of it) was established (1139). In 1147 Crusaders from

England, Normandy, the Low Countries and the Rhineland were en route to the Holy Land when they were persuaded to take part in the siege of Lisbon, which fell in October 1147. Pope Innocent III declared a Crusade in 1212, and months later the Muslims were decisively defeated at the battle of Las Navas de Toloso by forces from Castile, Navarre and Aragon, supported by Crusaders from France and Portugal. The only remaining Moorish kingdom was Granada, which survived until 1492, often due to masterly diplomacy and the payment of tribute. A further incentive was the marriage of Ferdinand II of Aragon to Princess Isabella of Castile in 1474. This formed an extremely powerful state, quelled the internecine struggles that that had so often distracted the Christians and led to the final downfall of Granada. Pope Sixtus IV had confirmed this momentous war as a Crusade, which greatly encouraged the participation of Christian warriors from the northern nations.

It is nearly impossible to classify the innumerable and wonderful castles in Spain into neat categories by type or date. We can see why this is so when we consider the

advances made by Christian forces across a broad front, extending roughly from east to west, and moving forward in stages at roughly hundred-year intervals, with a pause of nearly 200 years from about 1270 until the final downfall of Granada, the most southerly Moorish state, in 1492. In Iberia, Muslims were referred to as "Moor" more often than Saracen. Although both sides appear to have followed basic contemporary castle building trends, the specifically Oriental architectural influences seem to be more pronounced here than in the Holy Land. Possibly this is because the Moors had longer to develop a distinctive style of their own, and were the more influential inheritors of the skills and knowledge of the ancients, being Arabs rather than Turks.

Left and below: The Alcázar of Seville, while perhaps less striking than many other Spanish castles, is one of the most historic. Rumored to be the site of Julius Caesar's praetorium during his campaign in Spain, and showing evidence of Visigoth occupation, the core of this royal castle was built in the twelfth century by Berber (Almohad) invaders after their arrival in 1147. The huge walled precinct and some of the internal buildings still show traces of their Moorish origins.

Right: Baños de la Encina, Spain, guarding one of the passes that link Castile to Andalusia, was built in 986 on a high hill overlooking the town, and shows how advanced the Moors were in castle building compared to Europeans. It consisted then of a stout crenellated outer wall, set with fourteen square mural towers, enclosing a large area suitable for sheltering caravans or troops engaged in patrolling the highways and trade routes. A broad wall-walk was built around the entire circumference. In the thirteenth century, the area was finally conquered by Crusaders (c.1212), having changed hands several times before then. A large torre del homenaje *(keep), on the right of the illustration, was built into the walls as a sign of Christian victory, although it appears that no other permanent additions or alterations were made.*

The Norman and north Frankish influence on castle building appears less prominent here, in the earlier stages of the reconquest, than in Syria and Palestine.

The slow and overlapping changes in castle styles as the reconquest progressed mirror similar changes in other parts of Europe, for much the same reasons. There is now little evidence of the Christian defenses built in the north of Spain to repulse the Moors. Traces discovered in Asturias, Galicia and Leon, Navarre and Catalonia indicate that, as in the north, wooden palisades and ditches were normal forms of defensive structure. In the eleventh century, a stone tower, either circular or square, surrounded by a bailey and wall, was the type mainly built in the newly reconquered lands. This provided accommodation for the new lord, and protection for the peasants who were to farm the estates. A line of these castles, running from east to west, would mark the southerly extent of the Christian advance, and would also serve to launch new encroachments into the "no man's land" north of Moorish territory. These new castles would differ little from those in northern Europe: indeed, many Franks, Normans and other nationals would have flooded south once Iberian territory was there for the taking. Eventually, a form of hierarchy evolved, with the more powerful magnates gaining overlordship of wide tracts of the country, allocating estates to their vassals and collecting tribute, rents, tolls and taxes. An interesting feature here is that these later castles, as in the north, were furnished with tall towers to signal the administrative center of the lord's domain. In the role of donjon or keep, such towers were known as *Torres del Homenaje* (towers of homage), in which the vassal renewed his homage to his lord and submitted his taxes.

Castles built on crags and spurs were common, since these provided the best natural defenses against the Moors and greedy neighbors. Some would also be designated the property of the sovereign who ruled the newly conquered land and reserved for his visits. These would be larger and more luxurious, since not only did they need to accommodate a large retinue, they were also designed to impress with the importance and wealth of the owner. These lands, having been devastated by the struggle to reconquer them, had to be repopulated, and many castles were established as the

core of a fortified walled town or village that grew up around them. A breathtaking example of castle building, one of the most impressive features of Spain in the Middle Ages, are the *alcázars*, from the Moorish for fortified palaces. These were normally perched, as citadels, high above major cities, and when they fell into Christian hands they became, in turn, residences for Spanish royalty. The best-known are those of Seville, Segovia and Toledo. Although extensively rebuilt by their new Spanish owners, they still bear traces of their Arab founders. Of these, probably the most magnificent is the Alcázar of Toledo. Rebuilt by the Holy Roman Emperor Charles V in glorious Renaissance style, it fittingly symbolized the greatest empire of its time while retaining the imprint of its antecedents.

It is not surprising, since crusading offered the chance of gaining fame, wealth, influence and estates, that those warrior monks the Hospitallers and Templars would extend their exploits into Iberia and build magnificent castles in the process. A number of other fighting orders were founded to aid the reconquest, as well. The Knights of Calatrava, Santiago, Alcántara, the Holy

Below: The view from the wall-walk of the castle of Baños de la Encina, Spain.

Below: The view from the wall-walk of the castle of Baños de la Encina, Spain.

Opposite: Sesimbra (above) and Silves (below), two Portuguese fortresses that have common origins as Moorish constructions of the ninth/tenth centuries. Both have typically square mural towers and uncompromising crenellations.

Sepulchre and Montesa were all founded to this end. The renowned castle building of the Templars is seen in their strongholds along the Pilgrims Way, protecting the route to the most-visited destination for medieval pilgrimages, Santiago de Compostela. The huge castle at Ponferrada, in Leon, is a fine example of their skill and dedication. Other Templar castles are found at Gardeny, Miravet and Peniscola. As in the Holy Land, when the Templars were destroyed, their castles were taken over by the Hospitallers,

except for those that became Crown property. The Hospitallers are best known for their castle at Alcázar de San Juan, while the specifically Spanish orders left many traces of their buildings to be wondered at. These castles were, in effect, militarized monasteries, with little relation to the luxurious living styles that developed later in the castles of powerful magnates. Another addition to the various types of Spanish castle was the fortified monastery, occupied by monks of various orders that had no military affiliation. A beautiful example, Loarre (Huesca), belonged to the Augustinians. The monastery of Poblet boasts as fine a fortified gateway as that of many a military castle.

The buildings that have earned Spain the reputation of a land richly endowed with fairy-tale castles are, however, those that owe their almost magical appearance to Moorish architects. The Alhambra in Granada, last of the Moorish states to be reconquered, is known worldwide for its fabulous beauty, while it is also a mighty fortress. It must have served as a model for those nobles who wished to display their wealth and importance in a land where the Crusade had come to a triumphal end, but where danger from covetous neighbors or paranoid rulers remained commonplace. Many of the old castles that had nobly served their original purpose were left to molder on their mountaintops, but the more accessible were now restored, or rebuilt, with the help of skillful Moorish craftsmen. These were called *mudajjin* (allowed to remain) and stayed on after their Muslim rulers had been defeated. Their name was given to the *Mudéjar*-style castles built or restored for their new masters by the *alarifes* (masterbuilders) in the fourteenth and fifteenth centuries.

Although many of these castles were also influenced by the Gothic architecture that

had been introduced to France through contacts with Arab building techniques, it was the creation of exotic effects in warm, rosy-colored and highly decorated brick-work, and sumptuous internal plasterwork, that makes them so noteworthy. The finest example is the castle of Coca, in Segovia, built in the second half of the fifteenth century. It is truly magnificent, with a plethora of polyhedral towers and turrets. Its ground plan is basically simple: two con-centric curtain walls, surrounding square inner and outer baileys, each with towers at every corner. The inner curtain has a massive keep at one corner, and the wide, deep moat was furnished with two draw-bridges. There are numerous embrasures for firearms, fashioned of white limestone, and the walls, towers and keep are liberally decked with bartizans—small turrets that jut from a wall or tower.

Coca Castle
Segovia, Spain

Coca is a superb example of a castle-palace, built in the fifteenth century by the archbishop of Seville, Alfonso de Fonseca. The castle itself, stripped of its Mudéjar ornamentation and seen from a purely military point of view, is extremely impressive. Properly manned, it would have been assessed as impregnable by any experienced commander, which is probably why it was never besieged. Basically, it is a concentric, rectangular castle built of warm red brick. The outer curtain is broadly battered and set with semicircular mural towers. At each corner is a massive angle-tower/bastion, with gun loops covering the deep, brick-lined moat. The inner curtain has a huge corner keep of quatrefoil plan; the other three massive angle-towers are octagonal. The entire structure displays a fantastic array of molded brick crenellations and clusters of bartizans.

Left: The molded-brick crenellations, stone gun loops and multiple bartizans are all typical of Mudéjar architecture (an amalgam of Islamic and Gothic styles), as is the beautifully crafted brickwork, creating the impression of a structure glowing with warmth and light.

Right: A gun loop viewed from the castle interior.

Far right: The decorative gun loops at the higher levels, carved of limestone, were designed for handguns. The lower ones were for cannon, since fifteenth-century cannons were unwieldy.

CRUSADES IN FRANCE AND EASTERN EUROPE

Below: *This interesting engraving of the fabulous medieval walled city of Carcassonne does not do its subject justice. Much bigger than indicated, and more oval in shape, the integral castle is built into the center of one of the longer sides. The illustration does not show clearly the two concentric curtain walls surrounding the castle, each with many mural towers. Excluding the castle itself, the outer curtain had eighteen mural towers of various sizes, and the inner curtain twenty-five. The castle had a large circular barbican at the front, and a semicircular one at the rear. It is the most powerful example of a concentric fortification in the medieval west. It has been very well preserved, and was beautifully restored, if not entirely accurately, in the nineteenth century.*

The Crusade against the Cathars united nobles and knights from various countries in besieging castles and fortified towns, although it had more to do with the taking and destruction of castles than building them. The role played by Carcassonne, a fabled medieval castle and walled town in the Languedoc area of southern France, deserves mention here. In 1209 Pope Innocent III declared a Crusade against the Cathars, a heretical group that had established itself in southwestern France (the town of Albi was heavily involved, and so the members of the sect were called the Albigensians). It is interesting to note that this Crusade against fellow countrymen took precedence over Crusades against the Muslims, because of the politics between the French monarch and the Church.

A contemporary account tells of 20,000 knights and 200 foot soldiers marching into Languedoc in search of the rich pickings promised by the plunder of the wealthy lands there. The choice of a secular leader to head the assembled forces after the initial slaughter of the populations of Béziers and Carcassonne was Simon IV de Montfort, who had lands in the north and in England. By choosing Carcassonne as his main base of operations, Simon saved it from the destruction that awaited so many other towns and castles; today, the fortifications remain remarkably intact. After years of savage warfare, marked by unbelievable cruelty, a form of truce was signed in 1229 in the treaty of Paris. Nevertheless, the persecution of the Cathars continued, the Inquisition playing its full part after 1233 under Pope Gregory IX. The last Cathar bishop was killed by the Inquisitors in 1321.

The Teutonic Knights, also known as Knights of the Sword, were founded in the Holy Land in 1198. As an order of military monks, composed mainly of ethnic Germans, they were rather like a younger brother to the Templars and Hospitallers, occupying a single castle in the Levant. They supported the Crusade of Holy Roman Emperor Frederick II, the Great, and as a reward, were granted East Prussia in 1226. Soon they had conquered Latvia, Estonia and Lithuania, beginning the Germanic expansion to the east. Originally, the Polish duke of Masovia had used them as auxiliaries to subdue the Prussians, a pagan people, and convert them to Christianity. They concentrated exclusively on this Baltic crusade after the fall of Acre in 1291, and had conquered and occupied the whole of Prussia by 1283. Their massive fortified monasteries dominated the landscape, and they could be described as having carried out a form of "ethnic cleansing" to create land for German settlers. Eventually, they fell out with the Polish nobles, who defeated them in 1410 at the Battle of Tannenburg, while their efforts to penetrate Russia (Orthodox Christians were considered fair game) ended with their

Left: The walled city of Carcassonne is located in the south of France, its fortifications guarding the valley of the River Aude. Traces of late Roman and Visigoth foundations are still to be seen; the Saracens also occupied the fortress for a period. The stone castle was built after 1120 by the viscounts of Béziers, but the town, a major supporter of the Albigensians, was taken by the northern Crusaders in 1209. Simon de Montfort used Carcassonne as a base and thus saved its castle from destruction. The walls, towers, gates and barbicans were greatly strengthened by Louis IX. So famous did the strength of the castle and town become that in the Hundred Years war the Black Prince decided to bypass it.

sound defeat by Alexander Nevsky in 1242 at Lake Peipus. The order moved its headquarters to Marienburg in 1309, colonizing Prussia and establishing thousands of towns and many castles with which to control it. Free of the normal internal dynastic struggles and the internecine strife of medieval lords and barons (the monks were celibate), they were able to impose what is called an *Ordenstaat* (a form of religion-based totalitarian rule) over their lands. They gradually lost power, influence and territory, and when the Grand Master, Albrecht von Brandenburg, converted to Lutheranism in 1525, he secularized the order and became duke of Prussia: its castle building days were over. Still to be seen in what is now Poland are the massive castles of Marienburg, complete with the Grand Master's Hall (built 1380–98), and Marienwerder, to name two of the many that remain extant, despite the attentions of the advancing Russian Army toward the end of World War II.

THE HIGH POINT OF THE CASTLE

In looking at some of the most significant Crusades in the last chapter, we ran ahead of developments in the rest of Europe, in order to illustrate the interrelationship between the castles that evolved during the important conflicts in the heartlands and those on the periphery. It will be recalled that the first European Crusaders arrived in Constantinople in 1097, bringing their own several traditions of castle building with them. Over the next two centuries, there was a constant exchange of techniques, expertise and siege-warfare methods in general, and castle building in particular, between friend and enemy, and among allies. The many nationalities that became embroiled in this epic struggle all left their marks, and those that returned home soon set about translating their hard-won experience into stones (or bricks) and mortar. In discussing the main effects this had on European castles, we shall examine the major conflicts there to see why they were built. This is easier said than done, since gaining an overall view of European history during this period, with particular reference to conflict, could be compared to looking at a hundred television screens simultaneously, each showing a different soap opera, and then trying to narrate the story lines of only two or three.

It will be easier to look first at the parallel political developments in England and France, since they provide an excellent example not only of the need to build strong castles, but also of the underlying ethos of the times. An even better view results from considering the rise and fall of two main dynasties that played a major role in the brutal power struggles that typify this period: the Capetian and the Angevin.

Hugh, the first Capet, ruled a tiny country around the city of Paris, the *Ile-de-France*, but not Paris itself, and had very nebulous feudal links to other magnates who ruled in West Franconia, many of whose possessions far exceeded his. The name France for the nation came into use during the reigns of Hugh's Capetian successors in the twelfth century. The proliferation of powerful castles throughout the land has much to do with the way the country was divided, which also helps to explain certain episodes in the ensuing struggles. Castles could almost be described as symptoms of what we could call a disease: the overwhelming struggle for power and wealth that afflicted the medieval world and added incredible misery to the

already wretched lives of the people living in what is now called Christendom.

Charlemagne had ruled his huge empire firmly and allotted his trusted nobles large areas to rule in his name. They had virtually absolute authority over his subjects in return for their loyalty and support. These magnates, in turn, required support (military service, labor and taxes) from *their* subordinates. But over time, in the absence of a very strong ruler, the nobles came to regard their former areas of responsibility as their personal property. *Their* vassals, in return,

had seized seigniorial power and privilege for themselves whenever they could. The advent of primogeniture, as we have seen, created a very large group of trained aristocratic warriors with lances to sell to the highest bidder, or would-be plunderer.

Flanders, later an important ally of the Angevins, regarded itself as virtually independent, and its rulers became recognized as counts of the Holy Roman Empire in 1056. Catalonia originally formed part of West Franconia, and Aquitaine and Gascony were more aligned to Iberia than

Below: The Papal Palace at Avignon in southern France, although fortresslike in appearance, is more of a residence than a castle. Designed primarily as a symbol of power, it towers above the ancient walled city on the eastern bank of the lower River Rhône. The famous Roman bridge begins at bottom left. For nearly seventy years during the fourteenth century, French popes operated from this fortress-palace.

Above: *Kenilworth, one of the greatest castles in England, represents the second generation of Norman occupation. The land was given before 1125 by Henry I to his chamberlain Geoffrey de Clinton, who probably first built an inner bailey surrounding a motte, on which the stone keep was constructed before 1174. Henry II reclaimed the castle and improved the defenses: the large artificial lake was probably formed in this period. Sir Walter Scott based his novel* Kenilworth *on aspects of the castle's stirring history.*

to the north, while Normandy had its own views on its allegiance to the Capetian dynasty. In 1234 the counts of Champagne became kings of Navarre, and in 1261 the king of Anjou became the king of Naples. Burgundy had been divided into two parts since 843: only West Burgundy, virtually autonomous, had some loyalty to the Capetians, while East Burgundy looked to the Holy Roman Empire. Various local magnates were constantly competing for Provence, and in 1125 it was split between the counts of Barcelona and Toulouse. In 1225 the counts of Blois acquired the important county of Champagne, and in the Midi the counts of Toulouse dominated a very large area of southern France, stretching in the early twelfth century from the Rhone to Angoulême and from the Pyrenees to the Auvergne.

All of this helps to explain why every river and range of hills in France is graced either by the ruins of a medieval castle, or by a magnificently renovated and restored château, or "château-fort," a better translation of the word castle. These counts, kings and dukes warred with one another and with their vassals constantly, and the anarchy that ensued encouraged less powerful knights to enter the conflicts for what they could gain, and to use their castles as power bases from which to wring all they could from the lands that they dominated. This was not like the Crusades, or England after the Conquest, where a knight and his family lived surrounded by an alien and hostile population. This was their homeland, but without a firm, strong rule, castles enabled the proliferation of oppressive tyranny throughout Europe until their decline in the fifteenth century.

In England, by contrast, after the Norman Conquest, the many early castles built there left no one in doubt as to who ruled. William I's son (William II, called Rufus) fought a battle for the Crown of England and won, against the claims of his elder brother, Robert of Normandy. He ruthlessly suppressed several revolts and invasions. His younger brother, Henry I, who became king in 1100, was also a firm ruler, who finally united England and Normandy under his sway. This is a rare example of a case in which castles were the means of maintaining stability. Henry recognized the ongoing need to protect himself and his family, and built a residence within the bailey of his father's motte-and-bailey castle at Windsor. Briefly, England was spared the anarchy that was now rife in Charlemagne's empire, but when Henry died in 1135 a bitter civil war broke out over his successor. For twenty years, England was reduced to chaos. It was every man for himself, and many castles were built to defend often ill-gotten gains. Contemporary accounts tell of the dreadful plight of the peasants as the warring armies pillaged and plundered the land.

It was at this stage that a sea change in European history occurred, with a very significant effect upon castle building. To end the civil war, it was agreed that on King Stephen's death, Henry, grandson of William I and husband of Eleanor of Aquitaine, the discarded wife of the French king Louis VI, would rule. When he came to the throne, he reigned over more lands than any other monarch in Western Europe, his realm stretching from the Pyrenees to an indeterminate Scottish border, which he later defined. An iron-fisted ruler with an incredibly violent temper, he was also a great castle builder.

Henry II is remembered in England mainly as the alleged instigator of the martyrdom of the sainted Thomas Becket (1170), his talented ex-chancellor and archbishop of Canterbury, in 1170. But he also introduced the jury system and established King's Courts throughout the land, which severely limited the power of the castle-owning barons. He finally won his battle with the Church by insisting that the clergy should not be exempt from the king's laws, the cause of his quarrel with Becket. He also demolished the many castles that had sprung up during Stephen's reign and built, remodeled and strengthened many of his own. He enlarged the royal residence at Windsor Castle with a stout stone curtain wall, and in 1172 built the round tower there and divided the bailey into two wards with a strong partitioning wall. After invading Ireland and subduing its warring kings, he was recognized as Lord of Ireland in 1171, with the support of the pope. This would have interesting effects on the history of castles in Ireland, and was a reward for making the Irish clergy (Celtic Christians) submit to the authority of Rome, which they had resisted since 597.

In England, Henry constructed the massive keep at Kenilworth Castle, which has walls up to 5.5 yards (5m) thick, and square towers at the corners. His monumental donjon at Richmond, on the River Swale in Yorkshire, northern England, built within the earlier walls, was of similar rectangular design, with square corner towers. This castle has never been taken. To protect the crossing of the River Tyne at Newcastle, in northeastern England, Henry built another square-towered donjon to strengthen the existing castle; it stands some 28.5 yards (26m) high upon an artificial mound. However, his masterpiece was at Dover, the gateway to England. There had been a fortress here since prehistoric times, and a glimpse of the geography will show why the port on the coast nearest to France was

Below: The first castle at Durham, northern England, was a motte-and-bailey structure that was granted to the Bishop of Durham, a Marcher baron, in 1072. As at Canterbury and Rochester, a cathedral and castle stood side by side here. Early in the eleventh century, a stone shell enclosure was built on the motte, which was rebuilt in 1340. Successive alterations have transformed the castle during the centuries since, but the Norman chapel and parts of the keep have survived to this day.

a key location, while a site on the cliffs above was also recognized by the Romans as the obvious place to build a fort. Dover Castle has been occupied, strengthened, renovated and used for warlike purposes until modern times. It played a significant role in World War II, but Henry II's contribution is by far the most impressive. The truly massive rectangular donjon, with forebuilding, square corner towers and buttresses strengthening each wall, all surrounded by a massive curtain wall, cannot be missed by anyone approaching the English coast from France. It is interesting to note that the keep at Dover is often cited as typically Norman, when, in fact, it was built by the first Angevin king of England (whose family descended from the count of Anjou).

Henry's program of castle building and improvement extended throughout his empire. An outstanding example is his superb castle at Chinon. Sited on a spur overlooking the River Vienne near Tours, it consists of three distinct castles separated by deep moats. It later served the useful purpose of imprisoning his wife, Eleanor, for fifteen years after they had fallen out and she had encouraged his sons, Richard and John (made famous through Robin Hood films) to rebel against him. (This, of course, was long before the invention of counseling.) Henry died there, in misery and in squalor, in 1189, and Eleanor, although older, survived him for several years. Due to its commanding strategic location, Chinon was originally the site of a Roman fort, and had been built up as a strong fortress by the counts of Anjou. When Henry inherited it, he further reinforced it as part of a major reconstruction, with the addition of rectangular, semicircular and U-shaped towers. Later, it was acquired by the French king

Philip II (1205). During the reign of Philip IV, it was used as a prison for the unfortunate Templars after they were displaced. Here, too, Joan of Arc made her first, fateful meeting with the dauphin in 1429, during the so-called Hundred Years' War.

The great castle at Loche (Indre et Loire) also deserves attention. Here, Henry enclosed the castle with a curtain wall incorporating semicircular towers of equal height. Experts compare this with a similar construction in the earlier castle at Prague, which probably had an influence on it. Another example of Henry's work is found at Gisors, in Normandy. Here he considerably strengthened his grandfather's castle, built for William II, enclosing the existing keep with a hexagonal wall nearly 26 feet (7.9m) high, and supported with semicircular towers. Some of these were constructed in a novel way—*en bec,* or pointed like a beak in the direction of an enemy's most likely line of attack.

Henry II's elder son, Richard I, the Lionheart, was one of the most popular monarchs who ever ruled England, although in a ten-year reign he spent only seven months there. The rest of the time he was either leading the Third Crusade, or fighting to protect and expand the vast empire in France inherited from his father. His major work was a state-of-the-art castle on the borders of Normandy called the Château Gaillard, built on a 300-foot (90m) cliff above the Seine. Blocking the route from Paris, and covering the approach to Rouen, his capital in Normandy, it was built after the loss of his castle at Gisors between 1196 and 1198—a remarkably short time for such a monumental edifice. Château Gaillard took maximum advantage of its site on the river and the cliffs, making it a prime example of the lessons learned in the fierce sieges of the Holy

Land. There were three successive baileys, with moats between each. A circular donjon, built on the very edge of the cliff—the only possible approach—was shaped like the prow of a ship to deflect trebuchet missiles. It also deterred the use of a battering ram or sapping. This was one of the earliest examples of stone machicolations in western Europe, the supports for which rose from the splayed-out base, or batter. The inner curtain wall was not supported by wall towers, but its outer surface was

Above: Wooden hoardings, or brattices, providing a platform from which missiles could be dropped on attackers. This feature was the precursor to stone machicolations, one of the earliest examples of which augmented the defenses at the almost impregnable Château Gaillard.

corrugated, that is, it was entirely composed of adjoined semicircular towers to achieve complete flanking covering fire over the base. A strongly walled "new town" built on an island near the castle was reached by a fortified bridge from the opposite side of the river, and a stockade across the river, covered by the castle, not only protected its river side, but could block river traffic to Paris on the Seine. Richard was boastfully sure that his new castle was impregnable, and so it probably would have been, had he lived to defend it personally. However, he was killed accidentally while besieging an insignificant castle in an unnecessary campaign in 1199.

The story of Château Gaillard is closely tied to that of the French king Philip II, called Augustus. The epitome of a successful medieval monarch, he was an arch-plotter, as seen in his attempts to turn both Richard and John against their father and then against each other, and a good general. In 1198–99 Richard had defeated him with the aid of Baldwin of Flanders, and in 1202, after Richard's death, Philip took up the challenge against John, declaring him a felonious vassal for some obscure reason or other. (At the time, it would appear that every vassal could get away with being felonious if it were advantageous.) However, Philip now determined to rid France of the hated Angevins and started his campaign by besieging Château Gaillard. The fascinating military aspects of this epic siege (1203–04) are marred by the fate of some 400 wretched civilians who had taken refuge in the castle, but who were turned out when food became scarce, and they subsequently perished. They were halted by the French and forced to stay in the no-man's-land between castle and besiegers, in full accordance with the rules of war in those times. The siege had begun with the use of every weapon in a huge

armory. However, it ended, not with a bang, but with a sort of whimper. The outer bailey having been taken, a soldier discovered the outlet of the drain from the latrines, crawled up it, and gained entry to the middle bailey. Its wall was then open for mining, was countermined in turn and then collapsed. The castle was taken.

This defeat dealt a great blow to John's status, and to the morale of his allies and supporters, and marked the end of Angevin dominance in France. By 1206 Philip had won Normandy, Anjou, Maine, Touraine and Brittany, as well as Poitou and the Auvergne. The impressive castle of Angers in Anjou, although partially ruined, is still a formidable example of brute strength. The walls, constructed of slate bonded at intervals by sandstone and granite, were of a great height and defended by powerful towers placed closely together. Both walls and towers have widely battered plinths rising to half their height. Philip's expansion into Artois and Picardy led to a coalition between John, the counts of Flanders and Boulogne and the German emperor, but he defeated their combined forces roundly in 1214.

We shall now recross the Channel to look at John's plight. He was not regarded with much admiration and esteem by most of his barons, who had offered the crown of England to the French dauphin, Louis. At one stage, the rebels controlled almost half the nation. In 1216 Louis laid siege to Dover Castle, which was stoutly defended by Hubert de Burgh, the Justiciar. After a lengthy stand-off, the besiegers concentrated their efforts against the main outer gate that John had recently constructed at the northern end of the castle. They succeeded in taking the barbican (outer defensive works) and then directed a mine at the gate itself, bringing down the eastern of its twin towers. The defenders plugged the gap with

baulks of timber and continued their defiance until hostilities ended with John's death and the accession to the throne of his infant son, Henry III. However, it was clear that the castle was vulnerable to a sustained attack, and Hubert de Burgh was entrusted with the task of putting it right. At tremendous expense, the fallen gateway was rebuilt and a third solid tower *en bec* (beaked) was added to make up a trio. The massive Constable's Gate, completed in 1227, will be described later, when aspects of castle construction are discussed in more detail.

In France, Philip Augustus consolidated and defended his gains, strengthening many of the Angevin castles he had won with the help of knowledge he gained during the Crusades. These include the massive circular tower he built in the principal Norman castle of Falaise, from the walls of which the Conqueror's father had first seen the future mother of his illegitimate son. Centuries later, thousands of German soldiers became prisoners of war here after the invasion of Normandy. The famous castle at Loches also received Philip's attention: he added *en-bec* towers to the rectangular keep there.

In central Europe the Holy Roman Emperor Frederick II was a major castle builder of the age. He was a member of the Hohenstaufen dynasty, whose founder, the duke of Swabia, built the Staufen Castle in Swabia's Jura, thereby giving the family great status. The Habsburg dynasty, who became

Above: The Norman keep at Dover Castle is probably England's best-preserved example. It is the latest and largest of twelfth-century English rectangular tower keeps, rising on a splayed-out (battered) plinth to an overall height of 95 feet (29.0m), and measuring 98 by 96 feet (29.9 by 29.3m). The walls are immensely thick and are strengthened on each face by flat pilaster buttresses. Similar buttresses on each corner rise into the four angle turrets.

Dover Castle
Dover, England

The castle at Dover, on England's south coast, is regarded as Henry II's finest. Built on the site of a Roman fortification, this stronghold has been adapted numerous times to serve in a defensive military role for two millennia. The keep, shown below center, contains much of the castle's principle residential accommodation, including a basement and two stories connected by spiral staircases. The grand forebuilding has three towers and three flights of steps, which were originally open to the sky and covered by fire from the turrets. The Constable's Gate and lodgings, seen at far right below, were reached by a drawbridge over a very deep ditch, complete with portcullis. They are still the quarters of the current constable, a serving British brigadier.

Right: This turret at an angle (corner) of the roof of the keep provides access to the battlements by a spiral staircase from below, and contains the stairs leading to the sentry post on top of the turret.

Far right: This deep embrasure to a window illustrates the thickness of the keep walls.

Far right, below: A mural gallery in the keep walls, with a window on one side, overlooking one of the residential halls on the other.

Below: A view of Dover Castle showing its impressive twelfth-century rectangular tower keep, curtain walls and, at far right, the Constable's Gate.

Below: *Hohensalzburg. This massive castle is a symbol of the constant struggle between secular rulers and the Church during the Middle Ages. Pope Gregory VIII and Holy Roman Emperor Henry IV fell out over the issue of the appointment of bishops in 1077 and Archbishop Gebhart, a papal supporter, built the* Altes Schloss *(Old Castle) that year to secure a highway across the Alps. It has been enlarged continuously since then, notably by Archbishop Leonhard von Keutschach (1495-1519). In 1525 his successor was besieged here in the Peasant's Revolt. The outer bastions belong to the sixteenth and seventeenth centuries.*

Holy Roman Emperors in 1273, and who are probably the best-known family in European history, were named for their founder's castle, Habichtsburg (Hawks Castle), which overlooks the Aare River in modern Switzerland. And the Hohenzollern dynasty, whose name is not unknown in Germany, built their eponymous castle of Zollern in the southern Black Forest region with the help of Emperor Frederick I, Barbarossa, the famous Hohenstaufen who died en route to the Third Crusade, and who was the grandfather of Frederick II.

Crowned in Aachen in 1214, Frederick II, nicknamed *stupor mundi* ("wonder of the world"), saw himself in the role of a Roman ruler and left Germany mainly to fend for itself, granting virtual autonomy to the powerful German lords and the arch-

bishops of Cologne, Trier and Mainz. Frederick retained his powers by ruthless and well-conducted military campaigns when necessary, but his renown as a castle builder is due to the fact that he did not get on well with the papacy. His Crusade to the Holy Land, where he had himself crowned titular king of Jerusalem, alienated him from his spiritual lord. Frederick managed to get himself excommunicated three times, which could explain why he built so many exemplary castles in Italy, as well as invading the Papal States.

It is interesting that although Frederick's castles in Germany and Italy are called "Hohenstaufen," they are not similar. The Italian castles were architecturally more advanced than those in Germany, probably because they were built by Italian crafts-

Fortifications on the Rhine and Mosel

Overleaf: Landshut, dominating the valley of the River Mosel in Germany from its eminence above Bernkastel, affords a magnificent view from its *Bergfried* of one of Europe's major vineyard regions.

Below and page 97: Sooneck. Archbishop Willegis of Mainz built Sooneck Castle high above the River Rhine near Trechtingshausen. It fell into the hands of robber barons and was destroyed by King (not yet Emperor) Rudolf of Habsburg in 1272. Crown Prince Friedrich Wilhelm of Prussia acquired the ruins in 1834 and had them rebuilt in pseudo-Gothic style.

Gatefold: Burg Stahleck, dominating the Rhine above Bacharach, originally belonged to the archbishop of Cologne, but was handed over by Frederick I (Barbarossa, 1123-1190), to his brother, Konrad, about 1135. Konrad's daughter, by secretly marrying the son of Henry the Lion Duke of Bavaria, helped end one of the bitter dynastic feuds that marked the troubled history of Germany in those days.

Page 104: Reichenstein, above Trechtingshausen, is one of the oldest castles on the Rhine. It became notorious as the stronghold of robber barons in the thirteenth century and was destroyed twice, first by the League of Rhenish Cities in 1254, and again by King Rudolf von Habsburg in 1272. Like so many Rhine castles, it was rebuilt (in 1900) and now houses a private collection of weapons. (Note that the guns seen here are not of the Middle Ages!)

men and were affected by what is called the Cistercian influence. The Cistercians were an order of monks established around 1120, famous for building remote monasteries in an austere yet ornate Gothic style. They were very influential in the establishment of the Templars, who adopted elements of their constitution.

Frederick's castle at Bari was built on the ruins of a Norman castle, and when it was first constructed in 1233, it stood directly on the coast, which has now receded. It consisted of a courtyard enclosed by four wings, with a tower touching each of the southerly corners. There is a smaller hexagonal tower at one of the north corners, and a square tower at the other one; both are pointed. The walls are rusticated (rough-hewn), which was a Hohenstaufen trademark, and the sides that were not protected by the sea were ringed by a ditch. The corner towers were reminiscent of the earlier Norman castles.

The castle at Trani, also started in 1233, was enlarged and strengthened in 1249; it, too, has the four-wing plan with towers at each of the four corners. The largest tower is not fully integrated into the curtain construction, but merely touches it.

By far the most famous of all Frederick's castles is the Castle del Monte in Apulia. It is unique, which is rather a pity, since it has a beauty and grace—an almost ethereal appearance—seldom found in castles of that time. Sited on a small hill overlooking the countryside, its unusual ground plan is octagonal, with eight hexagonal towers with narrow loopholes projecting from each corner. The towers are of the same height as the curtain walls, which are exceptionally thick, as are the tower walls. Probably dating from around 1240, the castle has a certain spiritual quality that makes it easy to believe that some religious element was involved in its design.

Catania in Sicily also deserves mention. Constructed around 1240, it is rectangular, but unlike its Norman model, the corner towers are almost completely round, while a slender, near-circular tower protects the middle of each curtain wall. All the towers project above the walls. At Prato, in Tuscany, Frederick built a rectangular castle with corner towers that were the same height as the curtain walls. There is a tower to the left of the main entrance, with rectangular mural towers on two of the remaining sides. What makes this castle noteworthy is that the battlements have swallow-tailed merlons, as described below.

With Richard, Philip and Frederick, we have covered three of the four major castle builders in the twelfth and thirteenth centuries, when castle construction reached its apogée. Before reviewing the work of the other pre-eminent builder, who was English, we will turn to the rest of what is now known as Germany, where a wondrous array of castles sprang up. Although the kingdom of Germany was part of the Holy Roman Empire, it was separated from the other half, Italy, by the Alps. As we have seen, the Staufens focused on their Italian possessions to the neglect of Germany, where they had long depended upon the support of powerful dukes and counts, purchased by granting them virtual autonomy. Over time, this resulted in a period of virtual anarchy, when the Salian dynasty had to contend with civil wars and rebellions led mainly by Saxony and Swabia. When Frederick I, Barbarossa, came to the throne of the Holy Roman Empire in 1152, he had the strength of character to rule firmly, carved out a large imperial domain in northern Italy and was the epitome of the German urge to expand to the east, called *Drang nach Osten*, (later translated as the search for *Lebensraum*, or living space). He annexed Silesia and Pomerania and enlarged imperial domains in Swabia, Franconia and Thuringia.

Below: Schloss Heidelberg, standing on the banks of the Neckar River in the Palatinate (Pfalz) area of Baden-Wurttemberg, Germany, dominating both town and river, is a massive and imposing ruin. Once the home of the luxurious court of one of the Prince Electors of the Holy Roman Empire, most of its medieval origins (c. 1225) are now hidden behind the Renaissance palace into which it was converted in the sixteenth century, which, in its turn, has not recovered from war damage caused by French troops in 1689 and 1693. The round tower seen here dates from the fifteenth century. The protestant electors lost their homeland and title during the Reformation.

The twenty-five years after Barbarossa's death in 1190 were marked by renewed confrontations until the accession of Frederick II in 1215. His difficulties in controlling the vast empire he had inherited, due to his preoccupation south of the Alps, forced him to grant even more power and privileges to the German princes (including archbishops). Frederick's death was followed by what historians call "The Great Interregnum," which was caused not so much by the lack of a strong ruler, but by a surfeit of claimants to the throne, renewing instability in an already volatile climate.

For many reasons, the accession of Rudolf of Habsburg in 1273 has had repercussions throughout Europe for centuries. The Habsburgs, having originated in what is now Switzerland, were more concerned with consolidating and expanding their immediate possessions than involving themselves with more distant parts of the empire. Switzerland's abundance of crags and mountains was conducive to the creation of many beautiful castles.

During his reign (1273–91), Rudolf had moved his capital to Vienna, and acquired the duchies of Austria, Styria, Cariola and Carinthia after defeating the Bohemians in 1278: the castles in this area reflect these expansions. His death was followed by a new period of internecine struggles for the Crown, with Charles IV of Luxembourg deposing Louis the Bavarian in 1347. Charles moved *his* capital eastward to Prague, making it one of the grandest cities in Europe, as illustrated in a later chapter.

At this time most German castles featured a *Bergfried*, as we have seen. These were very tall towers, but not the equivalent of Norman donjons, since they were not designed primarily as residences for the lords who owned them. Later, when a curtain wall was built around the edge of the site, the *Bergfried* was moved closer to it, or completely incorporated into it: here the wall was made especially thick. Often, the shape of the castle was determined by the space available on the crag or spur on which it was built, which is why many ground plans are an elongated oval. Another of the features typical of the country was the *Schildmauer* (screen wall)—a particularly tall, thick wall barring the approach to the main building, which was often along a steeply climbing, sinuous track, protected by outworks. The enclosure would include a grand hall, or a suitable palace for rulers, and, of course, a chapel, which was often above the gatehouse. The proliferation of castles in Germany at this time reflects the fact that the many small states were often unable to impose their authority on their vassals or *Rittesleuter* (knights), due to inadequate resources for sustaining a lengthy siege. Another unique feature of some German castles is the practice whereby members of different families shared the protection they afforded. These were the *Ganerbenburgen,* or "co-inheritors" castles. An excellent example is Burg Eltz, where six *Häuser* (houses) lining the courtyard accommodated what must have been a pretty procreative aristocratic family. In what we now call Austria and Switzerland, the castles are, understandably, similar to those in Germany, many perched high on hilltops—naturally strong sites reinforced where possible to give the impression of serene impregnability. Particularly fine examples of the castles in this region are seen at Aggstein (lower Austria), Gruyeres (Fribourg) and Hochosterwitz (Carinthia).

Not every castle was on high ground. One of the world's most beautiful strongholds is on an island in Lake Geneva—Chillon, originally built in the tenth or eleventh century. Its mural towers are later additions, on the more vulnerable landward side. The castle was made famous by Byron's poem "The Prisoner of Chillon," based on the incarceration there of François Bonnivard, a Swiss hero. Habsburg Castle, near Brugg in the Aargau, is famous as the launching pad of the Habsburg dynasty. The *Bergfried* was probably built in the eleventh century, while the palace and curtain wall followed in the twelfth and thirteenth centuries. An archbishop built Hohensalzburg, another very famous castle, in 1077, during a period of instability. The Altes Schloss, as its name implies, is in the center, surrounded by many later additions and reinforcements, including the outer bastions dating from the sixteenth and seventeenth centuries. Dürnstein (lower Austria) is noteworthy on several counts. It was here that Richard the Lionheart was held for ransom by Duke Leopold V of Austria. Still an impressive ruin, it is built high on a cliff above the left bank of the Danube with its curtain following the line of the feature and outworks at the base of the cliff.

Schloss Heidelberg is not merely a famous tourist attraction. It was home to the counts of the Palatine of the Rhine, one of the seven Electors of the kings of Germany. Built before 1225, there is little now to be seen of the original castle, but the ruins provide fine examples of castle building from the thirteenth through the fifteenth centuries and into the Renaissance. The Drachenfels, on the Rhine, was built by the archbishop of Cologne, in his role as secular lord, in the first half of the twelfth century. Now in ruins, it is a reminder of

Above: Lichtenstein Castle, in Bavaria, Germany, started its existence as a Ganerbenburg, shared by the branches of the lords of Lichtenstein. The castle is divided into two. The ruined northern part, dating from the thirteenth/fourteenth centuries, had both a square Bergfried and a round tower, while the later, southern part includes living quarters with half-timbered frontages.

Below: Burg Eltz stands on a crag above the River Eltz in Germany. It is a prime example of a Ganerbenburg, *that is, it is split into several houses to accommodate the various branches of the same family. By 1268 the family of the counts of Eltz lived in the six* Häuser *that surrounded the courtyard. Not much remains of the medieval structures, except for Haus Platt-Eltz at the west end of the courtyard.*

the power exercised by such prelates in medieval times. The castle at Cochem, above the Mosel River, was probably built in the eleventh century and was enlarged when it came into the possession of the archbishop of Trier. Lichtenstein, in Bavaria, is another example of a *Ganerbenburg,* this one built to house three branches of the families of the lords of Lichtenstein.

The Rhine was the major route from the south to the north, from the Alps to the North Sea—the major artery of European civilization. The castles along the river granted their owners immense political and economic

power, the banks providing ideal sites for almost impregnable strongholds. The narrow gorge connecting Bingen to Koblenz (where the Mosel joins the Rhine) provided an ideal opportunity for control: there are more castles on this stretch of 35 miles (56 km) than on any other river in the world. We may recall that the Holy Roman Emperors had to shift troops and messengers rapidly between their possessions in Italy and their lands in the north. Who were the builders?

Between Mainz and Cologne there are up to forty castles, which gives us a clue as to why certain archbishops were given such privileges and extensive estates, including the archbishops of Cologne, Trier and Mainz—all members of the German College of Electors. These Rhine castles paid for themselves, and paid handsomely. Between Mainz and Cologne, there were no fewer than thirty different toll barriers, collecting dues not only from the river traffic, but also from the roads that followed the river closely through its valleys and gorges. Not all castles were owned all of the time by the archbishops: they could and did change hands. The Trier Elector, for example, originally built Elfeldt, now Eltville, but it was then captured by the Mainz elector. Rheinstein was built by Mainz, but Trier held it for a short time in 1350. The counts of the Palatine, also Electors, built and held several castles, as did the wonderfully named counts of Katzenelbogen, but the great majority were owned by the archbishops. Emperor Frederick I, Barbarossa, had given the Kaiserpfalz in Andernach to Cologne. These castles were held as fiefdoms from their owners, but the knights who occupied them regarded them purely as a means of enriching themselves. They soon became known as robber-knights, and were a serious threat to the flourishing trade that

would bring a degree of prosperity to Germany: "Rhenish" wine, for example was very popular even in medieval times. In the troubled period that preceded the election of Rudolf of Habsburg, the League of Rhenish Cities, in collaboration with the archbishops, set about ridding the Rhine of the plague of these robber-knights. However, from 1254 until 1272, when Rudolf himself took a hand, the struggle raged on. Imperial troops destroyed the castles of Rheinstein, Reichenstein, Sooneck (near Bingen) and Rheineck. Only one remained impregnable: Rheinfels, which was finally blown up by French troops in 1794 at the start of the Napoleonic Wars.

In the tradition of saving the best for last, the castles that Edward I of England built in Wales are unanimously regarded by the experts as by far the best ever built, measured against any standard. As a Crusader in the Holy Land, Edward had amply demonstrated his leadership capability, which so impressed the Muslim ruler Baybars that he arranged to have him assassinated. In fact, the English language owes a debt to Edward for this word. The Assassins were a tribe of greatly feared professional murderers who operated in the Holy Land. Edward himself, however, recovered from their poisoned-dagger wound, nursed back to health by his much-loved wife, Eleanor of Castile, who had accompanied him on the Crusade. He arrived home in 1274 (his father had died in 1272), having journeyed via Gascony, which was the only remaining English possession in France, where he proved his military prowess again.

Above: Burg Cochem stands on a hill high above its town and the River Mosel. Its purpose was to defend the town and collect tolls from river traffic, for which it used a stout chain from bank to bank. Built first around 1020, it was acquired in the early fourteenth century by Archbishop Baldwin of Trier, who considerably enlarged it. The medieval Bergfried, *Witches' Tower*, the remains of the main gate and a vaulted undercroft survived a major "restoration" in Victorian-Gothic style (1868-78), which probably accounts for the plethora of turrets and bartizans that grace it today.

109

Edward could feel secure on his throne because by now, in a world ruled from castles, those in his land were all held by his relatives and allies, if they were not royal seats, as indeed many were. In the absence of major distractions in Europe, the only potential source of trouble lay in Wales, Ireland and Scotland. The relationships of these three countries with the English monarchy were, at best, ambiguous, and Edward appeared content to leave it at that. The borderlands between England and Scotland—the Marches—were thick with powerful castles controlled by the strong "Marcher" lords, and the prince–bishop of Durham, who had his own private army, as did the other barons. Norman knights had penetrated these lands and built castles here, but they felt little allegiance to the English Crown. However, Edward could rely upon his trusted administrators, seneschals and constables—men of good birth but not ambitious landowners, who had been recruited from many lands for their loyalty and military skills, and who had served in the Crusades or in the barons' rebellion against his father, Henry III (1265).

One serious threat was posed by Llywelyn ap Gruffyd, lord of Gwynedd, the last of the quasi-independent "kingdoms" of Wales. His father had been killed trying to escape from the Tower of London. He had meddled in English and European politics, and, guarded by the precipitous and barren Welsh countryside in the shadow of Snowdon, he held a "royal" court and administered a "Welsh" law in his domain. The Welsh made fierce and destructive incursions into England, where they were contained by the Clares, Mortimers, Bohuns, Fitzalans and other Marcher lords. Edward regarded Llywelyn much as if he were an English earl, powerful and authorative within his own lands, but ultimately a feudal vassal of the English king. The solemn treaty made with Llywelyn, after the death of the rebel Simon de Montfort, whom he had supported, made clear that he owed his sovereign homage and fealty in return for being recognized as prince, or pendragon, of Wales.

However, Llywelyn wanted his relationship to the Crown to be similar to that of the Scottish kings: nominal suzerainty but completely self-governing. Ominously, he began to build stone castles without the king's permission, and Edward declared a state of war. He assembled a mighty, well-equipped army, including a thousand heavily armed horsemen, even more English and Welsh foot soldiers for use in terrain unsuitably for cavalry charges, and Gascon crossbowmen. Perhaps more importantly, he gathered a large fleet to support him by sea, to avoid having his lines of communication ravaged on land. Guerrilla warfare in their own territory was a method of fighting at which the Welsh (who had invented the longbow) were highly skilled, but Llywelyn, who had mustered an impressive resistance force, found that he was losing his allies as word spread about what they could expect from the experienced English commander.

In July 1276, Edward began his advance from Chester, reaching Flint, Rhuddlan and the mouth of the Conwy River within weeks. He then used his fleet to ferry a force that seized the island of Anglesey just as the harvest was being gotten in, thus denying Llywelyn his winter supplies. With his flank threatened from the sea, Llywelyn surrendered and threw himself on Edward's mercy. He signed a treaty at Conwy in November in which he renounced the claims he had made for privileges and territory, and swore fealty to Edward in Rhuddlan Castle, his base. This was originally a Norman motte-and-bailey construction, built in 1073 on the site of Gruffydd ap

Llywelyn's stronghold (our Llywelyn's ancestor) from which he would raid deep into English lands, thus fostering centuries of mutual esteem and regard. And now comes the reason for what some historians may consider an overreaction to this revolt. One could have expected that Llywelyn would have suffered a particularly nasty death: instead, during the Christmas feast in Westminster that year, Edward gave him the kiss of peace, agreed to his marriage with Simon de Montfort's daughter and presided over the wedding feast. All was sweetness and light. However, Llywelyn could not realize how well he had been treated, and persisted in demanding his "rights," which were concerned mainly with the fact that English law was in force in the Marches. He insisted

it should be Welsh law, which Edward's administrators regarded as barbaric, and his wishes were ignored. This he regarded as "monstrous injustice and affront." In 1282 he and his brothers launched an undeclared war, and a savage insurrection ensued. This was either a struggle for freedom from an alien yoke, or an act of foul treachery: Edward inclined to the latter view.

An even larger, well-balanced force and fleet were assembled again, and Llywelyn was swiftly driven back to Snowdon. But before he could surrender, accept the extremely harsh terms for a defeated traitor and throw himself yet again on Edward's mercy, a squire who had no idea whom he had slain killed him in a minor skirmish. Llywelyn's head was hacked off and dispatched to London

Below: Caerphilly, in Glamorgan, Wales, is one of the finest examples of a concentric castle in Britain, if not Europe. The castle is extremely well-defended: it stands in a huge artificial lake and has barbicans guarding the two massive gatehouses (see pages 84–85).

Above: White Castle in Gwent, Wales, is one of a trio owned by the famous Hubert de Burgh, the other two being Grosmont and Skenfrith in the same county. Work started on the site in 1161 and continued between 1184-85. In 1201 King John decided to strengthen the band of castles guarding the Welsh Marches, and he entrusted the three castles to Hugo. Massive angle towers were added to the twelfth-century curtain walls, and a formidable gatehouse built. When the work was finally finished, the design of White Castle, so called because it was whitewashed (as were most castles in those days), was well ahead of its contemporaries.

for display, and Edward set about ensuring that the Welsh settled down peaceably to English rule. The pre-Nazi German army had a saying: "Trust is good, but control is better!" Edward had tried trust, so now he designed a system of superlative castles and roads that would give him and his descendants control of these difficult subjects in their all-too-easily defensible country. The south was safely under control of his Marcher lords, so he devoted his efforts to the north. In fact, he began building the first of his chain of remarkable castles at Flint, after the first insurrection, which may have added to Llywelyn's sense of grievance.

Edward's chief master mason, Master James of St. George from Savoy, aided by master architects and builders from all over England and Europe, was responsible for starting the first two constructions, Flint and Rhuddlan. It is thought that his genius as a castle builder came to Edward's attention when he was crusading. Promoted to Master of the King's Works in Wales, he

supervised construction of the castles at Harlech, Beaumaris, Caernarfon and Conwy. Later, he carried out work at Lithlingow and other Scottish castle sites. The genius of Master James was that he could design the perfect castle for the strategical site on which it had to be built. Thus Caernarfon, with its castle-town, was designed to be the royal palace and administrative center for North Wales, while Harlech, another masterpiece, much smaller, was destined to be the dominating, impregnable and functional base from which the king's might could be imposed over the northwestern coast.

Work started on Flint on July 25, 1277. Traces of its town can still be detected. Remarkably, the castle's main feature is the vast, round donjon built as a flanking tower for protection of the gateway. This was out of date for its time, and is more similar to castles at Lillebonne or Aigues Mortes in France—well known to Edward—than the *dernier cri* in concentric castles he had seen in the Holy Land. The walls of this donjon are 23 feet (7.0m) thick, around a circular chamber 23 feet (7.0m) in diameter. The castle was completed in 1280, so rapidity may have dictated a simpler design.

Rhuddlan is an excellent example of the care Edward took to ensure that all his castles could be reinforced or resupplied by sea. A two-mile-long dyke was built, and the river diverted so that ships of forty tons could sail right up to the castle. An innovation in all of Edward's later castles was the provision of more than one gate and postern, allowing more flexibility in an aggressive defense, and, when necessary, a better chance for an evacuating garrison to fight another day. The lower outer curtain wall enabled defenders on the much higher inner curtain, and in the supporting towers, to fire over the heads of those in front, thus doubling the firepower that could be brought to bear on any point of the circumference. This style, now called concentric, was first seen by Western warriors at Constantinople in 1097, and developed further during ensuing Crusades. It is a good example of concentration and economy of force.

Edward started to build both Conwy and Caernarfon castles in 1283. Caernarfon's ground plan has been said to resemble an hourglass: narrow in the middle and bulbous at both ends. Surrounded by extremely strong and lofty walls, it had two massive gatehouses and nine powerful wall towers, many of them with turrets. The north side faced toward the new walled town, protected by a wide, deep moat, while the south side was on the bank of a wide river. Direct entry from the town to the inner bailey was provided by the King's Gate in the north, and the Queen's Gate gave access to the outer bailey from the east. Both these gatehouses were sophisticated and fully equipped. There were three postern gates from the inner bailey. Interestingly, one was from the great hall

in the inner bailey, opening onto the riverbank, for a quick getaway by water at need. Another postern was out of the Eagle Tower, a massive structure—virtually a keep—at the west end. This also opened onto the river. The third was in the northeastern wall tower, opening onto the moat. The southern walls, facing the river, had two tiers of passages (mural passages) built into the walls, each with arrow loops and holes through which to empty substances or missiles onto an enemy below. Thus three tiers of archers, including those on the battlements, could pour down fire on an assaulting force. Cognoscenti rank Caernarfon as one of the finest castles ever built anywhere.

Conwy Castle, built on a high rock on the shore of an estuary, follows the contours of the long, narrow eminence. This is called a linear defense, dictated, as in Caernarfon, by the site. A massive curtain wall surrounds it, with eight wall towers, one at each corner, and two in each of the northern and southern walls. There is a gate at each end—that is, to the east and west—and because the castle is so narrow, the northern and southern pairs of corner towers act as safeguards for their gates in the walls that join them. An outer defense work (barbican), east and west, provides extra protection for the gates. There are two posterns in the western inner bailey, where the royal accommodation was located, one requiring the use of a rope ladder to reach the river. Entrance was very difficult, recalling the Templar castles in the Holy Land. On the west, the town side, it was effected by climbing a steep stairway, crossing a drawbridge and passing through three fortified gates, all covered by fire from the walls and towers. To the east, from the estuary, approach was covered from the eastern barbican and a tower, no longer visible, was constructed in the estuary itself. The castle begun here in 1283, was almost finished by 1288. It was the

Overleaf: Caernarfon Castle, in Gwynedd, on the north coast of Wales, was not only a symbol of might and conquest: it was a statement. The finest of Edward I's great castles, it was intended to proclaim the permanence of England's hold over the recalcitrant Welsh. The banded masonry of its tremendously high curtain walls and the polygonal towers were designed to remind the Welsh of the power of the Roman Empire as embodied in the walls of Constantinople. Three turrets, each of which was crowned by an eagle, symbol of Imperial power, surmounted the largest of the towers, the massive Eagle Tower to the west. The castle was sited on the original motte of the first Norman ruler in Wales, Hugh, earl of Chester, who had built his castle two hundred years before.

Right: Corner tower detail of Caerphilly Castle, Wales (seen also on pages 84–85).

most expensive of all the exorbitantly expensive castles that Edward built in Wales, costing between two and three million pounds in today's money. It is recorded that in addition to James of St. George, the *supremo*, the best master craftsmen in the kingdom were employed: Richard of Chester, Henry of Oxford and Laurence of Canterbury. Because of its harmonious proportions, Conwy is regarded as the most beautiful of this group of extremely functional buildings.

The last pair of castles, Beaumaris and Harlech, are smaller than the others, but both are gems. Beaumaris, the last of the series, was built in Anglesey, an island off the northeastern corner of Wales, on the Menai Straits, the fertile "breadbasket" of the north. Constructed between 1295 and 1298, it is a superb example of the perfect concentric castle There was an outer moat, filled with controlled tidal waters; an outer curtain, equipped with turrets and loops;

and a massively fortified inner ward, the ultimate strength of the castle. This had a cylindrical tower at each corner, a D-shaped tower on each of the walls that did not contain a gate, and massive gatehouses in the walls at the other two ends—one almost a keep in its own right. Unfortunately, Beaumaris was never completed, since Edward's attention was diverted to the north. He was forced to move his operations to Scotland, where he earned the nickname "Hammer of the Scots." He had almost bankrupted his country in building these Welsh castles.

We have mentioned Harlech, another concentric castle, perched upon a crag above the seacoast and the estuary of the River Dwyryd. With circular turreted towers at each of the four corners of the curtain of the inner keep, and the outer ward a narrow platform hewn from the rock below it—just wide enough for defenders to man the battlements—it could serve as a model for what this type of castle should be. Building began in the early summer of 1283 and was completed by December 1290. By far the most impressive feature is the massive gatehouse-cum-keep, thrusting out in the only direction from which an attack could come. It consists of two great towers at each side of the drawbridge and gateway, and two slender towers flanking the entry passage to the inner bailey. It is satifying that Master James, "who translated into stunning achievement the king's will, desires and knowledge... was appointed constable of the new castle as a special reward for his services."

Below: Harlech Castle, Gwynedd, Wales, was built between 1283 and 1290 by Master James of St. George, who became its constable upon the castle's completion. Concentric in design, the castle has a combined keep/gatehouse and four cylindrical corner towers built into the inner curtain wall, and a lower outer curtain that included a fighting platform. The gatehouse walls are up to 12 feet (3.6m) thick; three portcullises protected the entrance passage, which also featured murder-holes in its ceiling.

Raglan Castle
Gwent, Wales

Raglan Castle is in ruins, but its story reflects the dramatic events that mark the history of England and Wales for almost one thousand years. The Norman lord William FitzOsbern built the first castle on this site, a motte-and-bailey structure, in the eleventh century, and his successors held it until it passed to William ap Thomas about 1405. William and his son, who became earl of Pembroke in 1648, prospered through their military prowess, wise marriages and support for the eventual victor in the Wars of the Roses. Raglan's palatial accommodation came later, with hexagonal towers, machicolations and the Great Gatehouse illustrated here.

Right: An elaborate decoration on a pilaster of a later building.

Far right: Stone machicolations built on decorated corbels on the fifteenth-century gatehouse tower.

Right, below: Possibly the walls of an earlier bailey, within which the replacement keep was built.

Far right, below: What was left of the "Yellow Keep" after Cromwell's forces failed to demolish it completely. It was probably a story higher before the prolonged bombardment of the final siege.

MAJOR DESIGN FEATURES

While location was the most important factor in the design of any particular castle, depending upon the type of terrain available and the proximity to the sea coasts, rivers and other bodies of water as well as towns and cities, other considerations and limitations affected the design. To name but a few: finance; time constraints; availability of materials, labor and skills; size of permanent garrison and peace manning; logistics; and purpose of construction. A few powerful and wealthy castle builders could discount many of these interrelated factors, but the majority of lords, bishops and knights embarking on building a new castle, or improving and modernizing an existing structure, would have to consider them carefully before finalizing the plan with their master builder. Inevitably, the result would be a compromise. Heated arguments about whether or not the budget could stand a barbican or an additional wall tower, or if a set of fashionable turrets on the gatehouse towers was really necessary, must have occurred before the first stone was laid.

Some of the limitations imposed by location are fairly obvious: carting vast quantities of stone up precipitous slopes posed a tremendous logistical problem, especially if it also involved the expense of transport from a distant quarry. It was a wise and fortunate castle builder who could build near his own quarry. The problem of supplies of all kinds for a castle set on a peak, far from track, river and cultivation—and there were many such—would make the prospective builder think hard. If he was concerned, as he should have been, with maintaining high morale among the members of his prospective garrison, he had to consider the problem of isolation as well as supply.

Finance was a top priority, especially as castles became more sophisticated and larger. By far the most expensive item, as it still is nowadays, was labor, and this tied in with the time of building required. If the castle could be built over a period of many years, labor costs could be reduced, but with the disadvantage that the structure would be out of date when completed. Edward I built his new castles, it seems, regardless of expense. His mandate resulted in incredibly fast completion dates, but accrued tremendous costs for the huge labor forces required. Records still exist for most of his Welsh castles, and it is no surprise to find that he recruited and impressed workers from all over England and transported them to Wales, where he had to house, feed and protect them. In a hostile environment, good protection during the building phase was a consideration often ignored by castle historians. The records for 1277 show that 300 carpenters from Derbyshire, 300 ditch diggers from

Yorkshire, 120 carpenters from Wiltshire, 120 masons from Dorset and 100 carpenters from Leicestershire were employed. This is a total of 500 carpenters for structures made principally of stone, and the list is by no means complete, as many other trades were involved. Harlech employed 207 masons and 115 quarriers, while at Beaumaris, 400 masons were assisted by a thousand mortar-and-lime mixers (skilled tradesmen), backed up by 200 carters. Smiths were needed to make metal tools and nails, and most skilled craftsmen made their own tools. At Beaumaris, Edward had to field 110 soldiers and twenty crossbowmen to protect the builders from the Welsh and to prevent pilfering. This makes it clear that Edward must have included "regardless of expense" in his instructions to Master James. It is difficult to equate medieval costs to modern prices, but it is thought that Edward's castles must have cost upwards of £3 million each. These figures give a rough idea of the costs

involved in castle building. Edward was a very popular king, backed by clever financiers, but even so, he nearly bankrupted England. There are many examples of less popular monarchs who faced revolt and revolution because they made exorbitant demands on their barons—often to provide the means of subjugating them.

Why were these costs so high? Because it would have been the height of folly to build a cheap castle. An "insecure" castle was a complete waste of money, and could seriously endanger the owner and his family. A potential enemy would be eager for any information about shortcuts taken to reduce costs, and any possible weaknesses. When we think of the great number of workers needed to build even a modest castle, such information would not be difficult to come by. Repairs and maintenance were also calculated in making the design, and it would not have been considered cost-effective to economize on materials and construction.

Below: The historic medieval city of Carcassonne in southern France provides a window into the turbulent past of that region. It is one of the few cities that has retained its concentric walls, that is, an outer wall much lower than the inner, allowing two banks of archers to fire on areas near the defenses. First built in late Roman times, Carcassonne was a bastion against the invading Moors and would have figured in Charlemagne's campaigns to establish a foothold south of the Pyrenees. During the Crusade against the Albigensian heresy (1209–1244) it was captured by Simon de Montfort and used as his base of operations. Seen here are some of the eighteen towers in the outer wall and the twenty-five defending the inner wall.

Below: The wall summits at Coca, in Segovia, Spain, showing the elaborately shaped brickwork that graced the late fifteenth-century Mudéjar-inspired Gothic structure. Combining grace and power, Coca would have been very difficult to capture if properly manned. Note the distinctive finials on the merlons, and the plethora of turrets, towers and bartizans that provide far more firing positions for defenders than would a straight wall.

Let us start by looking at a stone wall. Obviously, the height would be calculated on the purpose intended for it, and would also depend on current estimates of the likely threat. If there were such a thing as an "average" concentric castle, the outer curtain could be up to 300 feet (90m) long, up to 20 feet (6m) high and up to eight feet (2.5m) thick. An inner curtain would be higher, to enable archers on the battlements to fire over it—probably some 35 feet (10m) high and up to 12 feet (3m) thick. A curtain wall would have to be extremely stable, and resistant to efforts to undermine or sap it, which would entail digging very deep foundations, ideally, right down to bedrock. Deep foundations would also ensure against

collapse under attack by a battering ram, or repeated pounding with heavy missiles. Additional strength would be provided by a widely splayed base, or batter, which later evolved into a pointed buttress, to deflect the blows of the ram and missiles from a siege engine, as well as reducing the risks of undermining. As we have seen, a batter also directed missiles dropped on it by bouncing them outward toward an attacker.

Walls were constructed by building the outer and inner faces first. Materials, depending on location, could be limestone, sandstone, or ragstone (all called ashlar, from the Latin for "smooth stone"). In the case of a castle on the south coast of England, it could well be that the limestone used came

from the north coast of France, since shipping it would be easier and cheaper than transporting it by packhorse for long distances overland. Where stone was hard to come by, as in the Low Countries, brickwork was often employed. Mortar was a mixture of water, sand and lime—the job of a specialist, since its strength depended on getting the proportions exactly right. The space in between the faces was then completely filled with rubble mixed with concrete, and lengths of iron chain were often embedded to give it extra strength. The stone courses could be leveled off ("banded") with several courses of slate or tile, as in the walls of Constantinople, later copied by Edward I at Caernarfon. Scaffolding, another

skilled task, was used as the wall became higher and was often quite sophisticated. It was sometimes suspended from a higher point, or supported on beams projecting from holes set into the walls (called putlog holes) for this purpose. These can often be seen today in surving castle walls.

Once the wall had reached a certain height, the battlements were created on the outside of the walkway, or allure. Called crenellations, these consisted of alternating open embrasures and stone segments. The embrasures (called crenels) were often fitted with one or two pivoted shutters to provide extra protection for an archer firing at a target below. Originally, the solid sections, called merlons, were plain, but

Above: The walls of Baños de la Encina, in Jaén, Spain, seen here from the inside, were well adapted to the castle's purpose, which was to provide shelter for passing troops or caravans. It was built by the Moors in 896, with simple crenellations on the walls and fourteen square mural towers of straightforward design.

123

Right: This gateway to the Palace of the Grand Master of the Hospitallers, within the massively walled city of Rhodes, was built after the crusading order seized the island in 1310—probably after the earthquake of 1481. It illustrates an interesting stage in castle architecture in that its two semicircular towers are heavily machicolated and the merlons display elaborate and expensive swallowtails. It is surprising that there are no gun loops set low in the towers.

Opposite, above: The interior of the outer curtain wall of El Real de Manzanares, near Madrid, shows arrow loops set in alternate merlons that are also decoratively capped. The embrasures below are for access to the handgun loops that are set into the wall at about the height of a man. Framed in limestone, they also provide for a crossbow with their two lateral slots.

Opposite, below: There must have been very good reasons to justify the expense of adding merlons to the walls and towers of the Abbey of Passignano in Tuscany, Italy. The heavy machicolations on the crenellated tower indicate the expectations of attack, and the merlons are inset with arrow loops. The crenellated bell tower has no machicolations.

later they were often pierced by arrow slits, which slanted downward. Merlons could be square-shaped, which was the norm, or shaped in a variety of ways, including swallow-tailed (more often seen in Italy), or pointed. A merlon was usually as tall as, or taller than, a defender. An archer who wanted to fire directly down on attackers hard up against the base of the wall, or to hurl missiles down on them, would have to expose himself to enemy fire when he leaned over the parapet. To provide protection, wooden-roofed and -walled balconies were constructed, supported on beams projecting from putlog holes. These were called hoardings or brattices: they had apertures in the floor from which arrows and missiles could be directed downward, and arrow slits in the walls. The roof was covered with dampened hides to hinder attacks by fire. The summits of all build-

Above: A close-up of the top of a building and a turret of El Real de Manzanares, which was designed to be a magnificent palace. From a distance it appears to be strongly fortified, but closer inspection shows that what appear to be machicolations are two rows of decorative corbels, while the merlons—roofed over and decorated with stone tracery— are merely a series of apertures that were probably furnished with hinged shutters. The bartizans, lacking machicolations and arrow or gun loops to cover the faces of adjacent walls, are purely decorative.

ings, including towers and gatehouses, were made to allow the construction of brattices. In times of expected peace they could be dismounted and stored.

The provision of machicolations—a form of permanent stone brattices that served the same purpose—allowed the defenders to pour down fire and missiles on the attackers below. These were, of course, much stronger, providing greater protection against missiles and fire-arrows than the wooden structures. Built out on corbels (stone projections), they also enhanced the warlike appearance of the castle, and were much loved by Victorian copyists. They were especially desirable above a gatehouse, the castle's weakest point. One type used here was a form of chute, through which water was poured to douse any conflagration started

below by the enemy, in an attempt to burn down the gate, drawbridge and portcullis (which are detailed later). Although novelists like to describe the use of boiling oil poured down on the enemy, this is considered highly unlikely, due to the cost of oil. Greek fire, pitch and boiling water are more likely materials for deterring a foe who was too close for comfort. The keep at Château Gaillard, one of the sites where machicolations were used first, supported them on buttresses rather than corbels, but this limited the field of fire laterally.

Another feature typical of castle walls was the number of arrow slits, or arrow loops, as they were called. A tall curtain wall or tower might have as many as three tiers of these, access being provided by passages built into the walls. Originally, arrow

Left: This striking photograph of the tower at Medina del Campo, Spain, shows clearly the openings of the machicolations. The cluster of bartizan-turrets is typically Spanish and was reprised in the Victorian Gothic style.

Below: Herstmonceux, in England, is one of the first brick castles in the British Isles, with fine machicolations on stone corbels over the main gate. They are surmounted by merlons consisting mainly of stone arrow loops. The widely splayed triangular openings at their feet, designed to provide a wider field of fire, first came into use in England toward the end of the twelfth century.

Above: These arrow loops in Warwick Castle, one of England's finest, have a circular hole at head and foot and at either end of the cross slot, a feature that appeared first in the thirteenth century.

Right: A frontal view of one of the arrow loops in the outer wall of El Real de Manzanares, accessed by the embrasures seen on page 125. The square aperture below is probably a drain.

loops were merely narrow, vertical slits in the wall for an archer to fire through. Obviously, if they were high up, the bases had to slope downward, since a horizontal base would limit the archer to firing horizontally. Similarly, to enable a wider field of fire, the inner sides had to slope outward toward the walkway, to allow for an archer's lateral movements. For the longbow, a simple vertical slot was sufficient, particularly since this offered a minimum target to opposing bowmen or slingers. For the crossbow, a short horizontal slot was added, creating a crosslike aperture, and small holes at the extremities, called oilets, provided greater maneuverability. Later, a larger hole at the base was provided for the hand gunner, forming a large keyhole shape. Jumping ahead in time, it will be noticed that the wider embrasures for bigger cannons were often low in the walls—nearly at ground level—because if the barrels were depressed to fire downward, the shot would roll out. Higher embrasures, and those on the battlements, were provided for cannons intended to fire over greater distances. Windows, for light and ventilation, were narrow and placed high in any wall facing a likely enemy (called "the field"); the higher they were, the wider they could be. However, where they faced inward, and were set fairly high, as in living quarters or a chapel, they could be much bigger. Because of the thickness of the walls, a chamber, as wide as the window opening into the room, was needed: this was often provided with built-in seating banks to form a pleasant wall niche. Windows were normally protected by iron grills and shutters, but when affordable, glass windowpanes could be provided for the lord's accommodations.

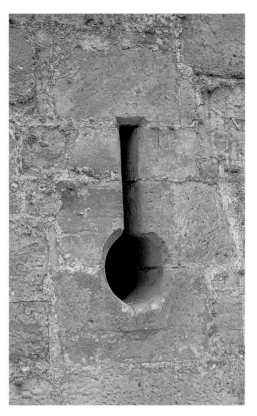

Left: This loophole in the walls of England's Bodiam Castle was originally designed for the crossbow, but was adapted later for artillery, as seen by the internal recess.

Below: These gun loops in the walls, turrets and many bartizans of the fabulous brick castle of Coca in Segovia, Spain, are obviously intended for handguns. Wider embrasures for cannon are seen in the bases of some of the bastionlike towers.

The castle's most noticeable and memorable features were its towers. We have seen that originally these were rectangular, and located at the corners of a rectangular donjon. They enclosed the spiral staircases that linked the various stories, and provided access to the roofs and turrets. We have also seen that because the corners of the towers, even those that were battered, were vulnerable to mining and sapping, circular or semicircular towers replaced them. These provided much greater protection because of their shape, like multilayered horizontal arches. Their disadvantage was that a round interior was difficult to adapt to normal usage for accommodation. The main reason for towers, aside from the extra height they provided for archers and petrariae, was that their projection from the walls, especially at corners, enabled flanking fire to be brought down along the entire face. If the curtain wall was too long for the range of the weapons in use, and to provide even more flanking fire, mural towers were built to project at intervals along the walls. In the concentric castle, of course, towers were a feature of both the inner and outer curtains.

Towers could be of two kinds: circular or semicircular. The former could become complete fortresses in themselves, with entrances only from the walkways or the ground floor and strong doors covered by arrow loops. Thus they could isolate any section of the wall that had been breached or scaled, forcing the enemy to go down into the killing ground between the curtains—the outer bailey. The walkways were reached by open stone or wooden stairways. With the doors open, defenders could rush through them to reach sections of the wall that were threatened. The circular tower, of course, also provided covered accommodation for many purposes on three or four stories. For purely defensive purposes, the

Above: The keep of the Alcázar of Segovia, Spain, has a dozen bartizan-turrets with deep machicolations between them.

Right: This crenellated tower of Warwick Castle, in the gatehouse complex, with its generous arrow loops and deep machicolations, dates from the fourteenth century.

Opposite, above: Enniskillen, County Fermanagh, Ireland, has two unusual narrow, tower-like structures on the corners.

Opposite, below: Access to Bodiam Castle in Sussex, England, was by a long bridge and drawbridge over the artifical lake, exposing attackers to concentrated fire.

semicircular tower, open at the back to the bailey, gave the same advantages as the round one: height and provision for flanking fire. The disadvantage was that, being open, it could not be used for accommodation, merely for shelter. The advantage, however, was that the rear provided no cover for any enemy who had penetrated so far. A curious and unusual feature of Château Gaillard was the construction of a curtain wall incorporating so many battered towers that they almost touched each other. This must have been immensely strong, and probably very expensive. Built by a king who was determined to have a perfect castle ("money no object" syndrome!), it is not surprising that this method did not become widespread.

Turrets, perched on top of towers, gave added height and were mainly used as watchtowers for sentries. The longest possible period of warning that an attack force was en route enabled the garrison to take urgent measures: recalling people from the fields, issuing arms from the stores, dousing unnecessary fires, lifting drawbridges, closing and barricading gates and manning the walls. Greater height also facilitated spotting the besieger's activities below, allowing fire from the castle's own engines to be directed more accurately at the siege-weapon positions. A well-organized castellan would have rehearsed this procedure often, using a trumpet call to sound the alarm. Smaller turrets jutting out from the corner of a large tower or wall were called bartizans. These, too, could bring extra flanking fire to bear along the faces of a wall and increase overall firepower, providing the garrison was strong enough to man them all. They were built out on corbels and seem to have been particularly popular both in Scotland and in Spain, as well as with Victorian architects. Access to the various floors within the tower was provided by

spiral staircases built of stone. They were so constructed that only an enemy's left hand would be free when climbing up, while the defender above him would have his sword arm free. Triangle-shaped stones were spiraled around a central post, called a newel, and slots in the wall allowed a little light in. Sometimes spiral staircases would be built *into* a thick wall, enabling builders to access the unfinished higher parts without using dangerously unstable scaffolding, while archers could access the mural passages. The towers were roofed with timber and lead, or, exceptionally, with stone vaulting. On the Continent, a conical roof was often used, as seen in illustrations for tales of knightly deeds. The layout of many towers was not dissimilar to that of a donjon. The ground floor would be used for stores, the upper floors for accommodation or offices. Where the tower was built on rock, an additional chamber was often hacked out underneath, with access only through a trapdoor in the floor above. A tiny channel cut into the wall or foundations would provide a degree of ventilation, but almost no light. This was the true dungeon, and a prisoner could get out only if a ladder was lowered to him; his food was thrown down from above. It was called the *oubliette* (French, which means "forget") for obvious reasons, and occasionally this space was also the cesspit. It is said that Edward II was incarcerated in a similar cell in Berkeley Castle in 1327, in the hope that he would catch some terminal disease from the effluent. When he survived this, he was murdered on the instructions of his wife.

As we have seen, castle walls became so strong and well defended that an attacker perceived the main gate as the most vulnerable point and concentrated his efforts here. The reaction to this was an immense strengthening of the entire approach and entrance to the castle. The main gate was often directly by a tower, or even in a tower, and provided with machicolations above it. A drawbridge across the moat or ditch, when it was raised, made it difficult to reach the gate. However, this proved inadequate against a determined attack by a well-equipped and powerful enemy, and the concept of the gatehouse evolved. Eventually, it became a mini-castle in its own right. One of the strongest gatehouses was that in Edward I's Harlech Castle. A typical later-medieval gatehouse consisted of an extremely strong, rectangular, three-storied building with a tower at each corner, the two in the bailey probably rather less massive than the two outside. The towers would be crenellated and provided with arrow loops, directed mainly at the gate itself. Machicolations were positioned above both front and rear (there were often two) gates, and often on all the towers. We have mentioned the chute, or shoot, often engineered to provide the means of dousing a

Opposite: *The modest gate to El Real de Manzanares. The absence of a gatehouse-keep, with barbican, portcullis and drawbridge, reminds us that this palace was not designed to withstand a long siege. By contrast, the gatehouse to the thirteenth-century White Castle, Wales (below), was equipped with massive flanking towers above the steep slope to the moat.*

Left and below: *These two portcullises—at Coca (left) and Bodiam (below)—are made of heavy wood and tipped with steel, providing strong barriers. In castles with two or more portcullises, attackers trapped between them could be destroyed through murder-holes in the gateway roof and arrow loops in the interior sidewalls.*

Above: A view of the fourteenth-century barbican of Warwick Castle showing the silhouette of a raised portcullis. This was first of several barriers an attacker faced to gain entry.

and having iron spikes on their lower edges. Set in grooves cut into the sides of the passage walls, they were raised by means of windlasses, often operated from different stories above. When released, they clashed down, spearing any attacker caught below. One or more drawbridges were set into the gateways, often at each end and sometimes over a pit in the passage itself. Originally, the bridge was drawn up from its horizontal position over the moat or ditch by chains operated by a windlass above the gate. This could be a lengthy and strenuous process, and it was often replaced by a system using pivoted counterbalanced beams. The bridge was attached by chains to the ends of the beams, which, when released, rose and fitted into recesses above the gateway, the counterweighted ends sinking into a pit. Sometimes pedestrians were provided with a narrower drawbridge of their own, worked on the same system. Another very similar, but simpler, system was to pivot the entire bridge on an axle, rather like a seesaw, with the inner end weighted and supported on a movable stop. When the stop was withdrawn, the weighted end dropped into a pit below, while the lighter end swung up and formed still another obstacle. The passage itself was lined with arrow loops, enabling archers in the ground floors of the towers (often called guard rooms) close-range shots at the invaders, while holes in the roof (aptly called murder-holes, and sometimes machicolations), allowed defenders in the upper stories to pour down boiling water, pitch or anything else that could kill or impede those below. They could also be used to supplement or replace the water-shoots described above. Those passages that widened out into a two-story-high chamber halfway along their length exposed an advancing enemy to fire and missiles hurled by defenders from open doorways in the tower chambers above.

fire built to burn down the gate. The gate(s) would be of thick oak planks, reinforced with iron strapping, and secured with beams let into the walls at either side, called draw-bars. Many castles, especially in Scotland, would also be equipped with an iron "yett," a heavy gate formed as a grill, with two leaves. The gateway itself was, in effect, a long passage, which could widen out into a two-storied chamber halfway along. Portcullises—there could be two or three—were heavy, ponderous, wooden grids strengthened with iron

Very often it was the practice to build yet another defensive structure outside and in front of the gateway, making approach more difficult and imposing delay on an attacker. This was the barbican—a walled outwork, often including machicolated towers, one or more drawbridges and portcullises. It could, and often did, duplicate most of the features of the main gatehouse, and was usually on the enemy side of the moat or ditch, guarding a bridge or causeway across it. There it played a role in guarding the berm—the land between the outer curtain and the moat. Sometimes a shield wall would serve this purpose. In hill country, the approach to a castle was often via a narrow, steeply climbing, sinuous track: here, barbicans and defended outworks were positioned at key points for halting an advance. In a concentric castle, gatehouses were built into both outer and inner curtain walls; the inner one was usually the stronger. As mentioned earlier, many castles were built with sally ports, which allowed the defenders to mount a sudden surprise attack, killing as many invaders as possible, destroying their siege engines, then rushing back inside. Sally ports also enabled a discreet evacuation if needed. Where the castle walls adjoined a coast or waterway of some kind to enable a getaway by boat, a sally port was often associated with a water gate and pier, where a smaller gatehouse and barbican, or some other outwork, offered further protection.

Not much has been said so far about living accommodations for lord and garrison: most domestic arrangements will be described later. However, exploring castle construction, we may look at some non-military, but essential features. The first item is the Great Hall required in every castle. Indeed, it could be said that the castle existed to protect this, certainly in the early days. Starting with the donjon, one upper story would be devoted to eating and sleeping for the whole garrison, the lord and his family having some privacy in one or more small chambers opening out from it, called the solar. Later, a freestanding Great Hall, roofed not with rushes, but with tiles or slates as a precaution against fire-arrows, would be constructed within the inner bailey. This would not always be built of stone; it could well be of timber and serve the whole garrison. With the advent of the concentric castle, the Great Hall would often

Below: The original thirteenth-century gatehouse of Cahir Castle, County Tipperary, was converted into a Great Tower (keep) during fifteenth-century reconstructions and enlargement. A smaller gateway created nearby, which fronted the portcullis seen here, had a double-arched head.

Right: Few British castles are more familiar than Edinburgh, which reflects the turbulent history of Scotland. It towers above the capital city on a huge rock-face that looms some 270 feet (82.3 m) high. A castle has stood here since Malcolm III built his wooden fortress in the eleventh century, but few traces remain of the medieval buildings that have been replaced by later defenses and accommodations. At the summit is the chapel named for St. Margaret, Malcolm's queen, which retains some traces of its earlier origins. David's Tower, named after its builder David II and constructed 1368–71, was largely destroyed in the siege of 1583. Perhaps the best-known incidents in the castle's history are its capture by Edward I of England, called the "Hammer of the Scots," in 1296, and its recapture in 1313 by Robert the Bruce's nephew, Thomas Randolf, Earl of Moray.

be built against the inner curtain; if located in a corner, only two sides had to be constructed, often of wattle and daub.

A gatehouse with ample accommodation in its upper stories could well be the domestic quarters of the castellan, for several reasons. Living above the main gate, he and his immediate household could guard against treachery; in the case of an enemy break-in, this was probably the safest place in the castle from which to operate the defense, since it provided protection from both front and rear; in an age when more and more soldiers were mercenaries, their loyalty could not always be counted on in the face of deteriorating conditions, bad morale, or a better offer from the foe.

Not all castles were concentric, and later ones that had only one curtain wall (called linear or rectangular), would have their walls lined with substantial buildings facing the courtyard. This provided a kind of double wall: if an attacker did breach the curtain, he would find himself in a substantially enclosed "room," from which he had to fight his way out. If the Great Hall was two-storied, access to the upper story would probably be by an external open staircase. Heating was provided by open fireplaces, and chimney shafts built into the walls replaced the earlier holes in the roof.

A separate kitchen was built near the Great Hall to reduce the risk of fire, and the well (one of the castle's vital features, for obvious reasons) was as near as possible. The well in Dover Castle keep, for example, is fabulously deep, and provided water to various parts of the keep through lead pipes. There was also a cistern here for collecting rainwater, as in Crusader castles and the ancient fortresses of the Middle East, where such cisterns were essential. The kitchen of a king's castle had to be very large to cater for customary banquets and feasts.

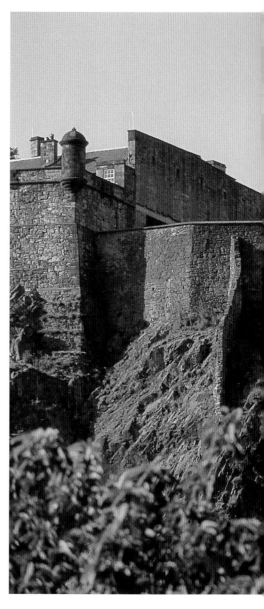

With so many people crammed together, and the constant threat of fearful diseases, hygiene would always be considered by the experienced builder. Bathing was common, despite popular belief, but it was only the very wealthy owner who could afford a bathtub in his living quarters. Bathing facilities were usually inside the kitchen, where large quantities of water could be heated up. Attention was also given to the location of latrines. Called garderobes, they were situated either above or alongside drainage shafts built into the outside walls, and emptied into a cesspit or discharged into the moat.

Another method was to project the garde-robes from the curtain wall, supported on corbels, rather like brattices or machicolations. One writer complained that the aesthetic beauty of the whitewashed castle (most were whitened—hence the "white tower" of the Tower of London) was spoilt by the obvious traces of their function that decorated the walls below them. (It must be supposed that these small rooms were not popular when a castle was undergoing a bombardment by heavy siege weapons.)

It is interesting to note in passing that the Teutonic Knights invented their own unique system of hygiene. Since, as a monastic body, they spent most of their time in communal pursuits, attending the many services that filled the days and nights, and eating together in their refectories, they were also required to attend to the needs of nature at the same limited time. Medieval monasteries are known for their many-seated *necessariums*, but the Teutonic Knights built large privy-houses high above a river or moat, connected to the main building by a long covered passage supported on lofty arches. This was called a *Danziger*, for the port of Danzig that they had conquered, but no one seems to know why.

CHANGE, DECLINE
AND RENEWAL

Having described the castles built by Edward I of England as the high point of castle building, we might assume that the story ends with the destruction and ruin of these once-proud symbols of feudal dominance. Many books on the subject draw this erroneous conclusion, but castles continued to play a role during the late Middle Ages, although a different and less essential one. A look at the interrelated political, economic and social changes that began to take place throughout Europe helps explain how castles were affected, although space allows us to unravel only a few threads of this complicated pattern. The expansion eastward continued, and in many lands dynastic wars and internecine strife were just as brutal and vicious as they had ever been, and with new threats appearing on shifting borders.

It is always fascinating to look back in time and learn more about the attitudes first-hand. A pertinent paragraph in Niccolo Machiavelli's *The Prince*, chapter 10, gives a telling insight into complex four-teenth-century politics:

And whosoever shall fortify his town well...will never be attacked without great caution, for men are always adverse to enterprises where difficulties can be seen, and it will be seen not to be an easy thing to attack one who has his town well fortified and is not hated by his people.

The cities of Germany are absolutely free, they own but little country round them, and they yield obedience to the emperor when it suits them, nor do they fear this or any other power they may have near them, because they are fortified in such a way that everyone thinks the taking of them by assault would be tedious and difficult, seeing they have proper ditches and walls, they have sufficient artillery, and they always keep in public depots enough for one year's eating, drinking and firing. And beyond this, to keep the people quiet...they always have the means of giving work to the community in those labors that are the life and strength of the city.

From this we learn that it was considered important, even then, to have popular support, ensured by worthwhile employment in industry and commerce. This created wealth, which people were prepared to defend energetically. Also significant is the fact that Machiavelli singles out the town rather than the prince's castle, and that he uses Germany as an example, and not the city-states of his native Italy, which figured largely in the European balance of power. It was Pisa's fleet that drove the Saracens from Sardinia in 1016, and in 1063 sacked Palermo, then a Muslim city. Genoa supplied many of the ships used to transport the early Crusaders to the Holy Land, thus earning special trading privileges. By 1300 Genoa was one of the largest cities in Europe, with a population of a hundred thousand. The Fourth Crusade (1204), which captured Constantinople, was inspired and financed by Venice, and was rewarded with three-eighths of the former Byzantine Empire and many treasures, including four bronze horses displayed in Venice today. The Crusaders could not have survived in their Palestinian coastal towns and castles if the fleets of these merchant-states had not supported them. Florence, the home of Machiavelli, fought regularly with Pisa and Milan, and from 1427 competed with Genoa and Venice for Mediterranean trade. These facts illustrate that commerce was becoming a major factor in the medieval political scene, and that trade and industry fostered the emergence and growth of cities.

The Black Death, which struck Europe in 1348, had many significant consequences, apart from the obvious and immediate ones. A good example is the Peasants' Revolt in England in 1381. Richard II, son

Previous pages: Castle Campbell was built by the powerful Campbell clan near the town of Dollar, in central Scotland. The impressive tower-house is sited on a spectacular rocky spur with steep cliffs on all sides; the "Burn (river) of Sorrow" flows along one side, and the "Burn of Care" on the other. Dating from the fifteenth century, the tower-house is some 60 feet (18m) high to the machicolated parapet, and has four stories, with a pit prison in the basement. Increasing wealth and grandeur enabled the Campbells to expand their stronghold in the sixteenth century to a massive courtyard castle. The castle was damaged by fire during the English Civil War, but the tower has survived well.

of the Black Prince, was a 14-year-old boy when his government imposed a head or poll tax that penalized the powerless peasantry. A popular uprising in southeastern England ended in the fall of the Tower of London by deceit, and the execution of the Chancellor, who was also the Archbishop of Canterbury, and the Royal Treasurer. The peasants had realized that the Black Death had so diminished the population that their labor was worth more than the bare subsistence they had scratched out under the feudal system. Landowners competed for labor, paying wages that became inflated due to rising demands. The concept of feudal duties dwindled, and the end of serfdom was in sight, since serfdom was the basis of feudalism: the possession of land was worthless without the labor to work

it. If kings and magnates wanted to wage war, or to defend their lands, they would have to pay soldiers—the mercenaries—and pay them well. We have already seen, briefly, how this affected the design of a castle, via the threat of treachery or mutiny from unreliable mercenaries and the need to provide extra protection for the owner or castellan. At the outset, the peasants did not "hate" their young king, but they may well have done so after he reneged on his promise to consider their grievances, and they were brutally suppressed.

In mentioning Richard II, we bring up the Hundred Years' War between England and France (1337–1445). This period of sporadic warfire consisted of sieges, raids, sea battles and occasional land battles, with long intervals of uneasy truce. One cause

Below: This massive gateway (the Holstentor) to the old town of the German city and port of Lübeck, Schleswig-Holstein, tells its own part of the story of the castle. Built in 1477, the edifice was intended to impress, emphasizing the city's riches and independence: the elaborate artwork and Gothic windows on the town side would have added little to its effectiveness as a defense. It was a symbol of the rising power and wealth of great European cities, which depended on trade for their existence, and a sign that the mastery of the feudal lord and his castle were over.

Right: Craigievar Castle stands some 300 feet (90m) below the 1000-foot (300m) summit of a hill in Grampian, Scotland. Although its origins lie in the mid-thirteenth century, the extant L-plan building was constructed at the end of the sixteenth century by the Mortimer family. Before it was finished, the estate was bought by the neighboring Forbes family and completed in 1626. The castle has been in continuous occupation ever since, with additions and alterations reflecting changes in taste over the years. It now has seven stories and finely corbelled cylindrical bartizan-type turrets with conical roofs. The entrance is through a massive iron-studded door protected by a yett.

was England's desire to control Flanders, the major buyer of wool, its main export, which highlights the growing importance of commerce. The first phase of the war saw the Battle of Crécy in 1346, wherein a greatly outnumbered English force of long-bowmen slaughtered the exemplars of French chivalry—heavily armored mounted knights. This was followed (1347) by the siege and capture of Calais, a well fortified and stoutly defended port city that saw one of the first recorded uses of cannon in European warfare. The Black Death ended hostilities for a time, and the next phase brought England's Edward, Prince of Wales (called the Black Prince), into prominence. He commanded the English invasion of southern France and in 1356 used his bowmen again to defeat a much larger force of French knights, taking the French king and many wealthy lords for huge ransoms. The English claim to Aquitaine was reinforced, and the rich region was ceded to him by his father, Edward III. The Black Prince ruled here until 1371, when an uprising in Limoges,

caused by prohibitive taxation, was put down at a great cost in lives and money, and he returned to England. He died there five years later, having unwittingly proved that the cost of making war had doubled in the wake of the Black Death.

By 1374 English possessions in Aquitaine had shrunk to little more than the towns of Bordeaux and Bayonne, and the fighting had shifted to Brittany and Normandy. In 1415 Henry V of England demonstrated again, with a victory over the French at Agincourt, that the total supremacy of the mounted knight and his stronghold were waning. It was the strongly fortified and defended towns, not individual castles, that were besieged, captured, or bypassed.

John Keegan, the renowned military historian, has made an important point about fifteenth-century warfare. Although cannon may have been used at Agincourt, they made little, if any, impression, and he observes that, forty years later, when the English were finally expelled from Normandy and Aquitaine in the campaigns of 1450–53, "They knocked through castle walls of the English strongholds with cannon; at exactly the same time the Turks were battering down the walls of Theodosius at Constantinople with monster bombards." In 1478 Louis XI of France extended his area of control over his ancestral lands by using cannon against the castles of the dukes of Burgundy. This resulted in the French king's gaining full control of his own land for the first time in six centuries: he could exercise central government—"supported by a fiscal system in which cannon were the ultimate tax collectors from refractory vassals." This marks the end of the feudal system and of the semiautonomous baron. He could no longer engage in internal power politics and plot against his liege lord from the safety of the impregnable castle.

The age of the siege cannon had arrived. Only a king could afford to own and deploy a powerful siege train: slow and cumbersome it may have been, but a castle was not going to run away. Many consider the end of the

Hundred Years' War synonymous with the beginning of nationalism in both countries. And although France became united under a firm rule, in England the Wars of the Roses (1455–85) proved that internecine strife was not dead and that the castle was still an important factor in major civil wars. Essentially, however, its design did not change from that of the massive, sophisticated stronghold of the late thirteenth century. It was not until the first Tudor, Henry VII, won his crown at the Battle of Bosworth in 1485, that an English king could concentrate on building defenses to keep his enemies out without major distraction from the threat of enemies within, or the desire to regain lost lands in France. Rulers no longer had to pander to powerful subordinates: many castles that could be considered threatening were demolished and new ones were prohibited.

Scotland is a fruitful field of study, for it seems that there is seldom a period in which that country enjoyed universal peace.

Below: Stirling Castle, the "Gateway to the Highlands," in Grampian, is one of the most famous royal Scottish castles. Built on the site of a timber-and-earthwork structure, the castle is perched on a great basalt rock some 250 feet (76m) high. That nothing remains of the many fortifications built before the fifteenth century says much about its violent history. The best-known episode in its long record of conflict is the ignominious defeat of the anti-warrior King Edward II of England, at nearby Bannockburn in 1314.

Above: There can be few castles as famous as that at Edinburgh, whose history encapsulates the stormy and bloody history of Scotland. Built on the precipice of an extinct volcano, it towers 270 feet (82.3m) above the capital. The only trace of the wooden castle King Malcolm III built here is the chapel of his queen, St. Margaret, where she died in 1093. Robert the Bruce's son David II substantially refortified the rock on his succession in 1329, covering the more vulnerable approaches with stout walls. Traces can still be seen of David's Tower.

The Scots fought the English, the French, and each other, which explains the many castles—and ruins—throughout its beautiful landscape. The Romans never succeeded in occupying Scotland, although their legions penetrated as far north as the River Forth. Apparently, the premedieval fortresses were of the hilltop variety, whereby a terrace round a crag or prominence—of which there is no lack—supported a wall of stone, or stone and timber. A breastwork on the terrace completed a formidable defense.

In the north, the Outer Hebrides, Orkney and Shetland developed unique structures called *brochs*. These were circular in plan, with an internal diameter of about 25 feet (7.5m) and walls up to 16 feet (4.9m) thick. Some were so high that they could be called towers. Sidney Toy, an expert castle historian, gives this description: "Two concentric shells, tied together at intervals by long stones. The outer shell is steeply battered, while the inner one is practically vertical. The most perfect example of a tower broch is at Mousa, in Shetland, which still stands to the height of about 45 feet (13.7m). Its outer wall is unbroken by any aperture save for the doorway on the ground floor, but four series of slits run up the inner wall. Chambers, stairways, and galleries are formed in the space between the shells."

The Scots also protected their towns and settlements in the same way as the Saxons in the south, building a double stone wall filled with rubble around them. The walls were tied together with wooden beams, or strengthened with timber, and it is a poignant reminder of Scotland's stormy past that many of the remains of these fortifications are called "Vitrified forts," since they appear to have been destroyed by fire, fusing the core. Many Scots would claim even today that Scotland has never been truly united, with an obvious distinction between the Celtic (or Gaelic) peoples of the Highlands and the Saxon, Danish and Norman folk of the Lowlands.

The Scottish king Malcolm II, a contemporary of the Danish king of England, Canute, wrested Lothian, the lands around what is now the city of Edinburgh, from its English/Danish earl and annexed it to his own kingdom. This area became politically predominant, and was regarded by the English as Scotland, while to the Gaels it remained *Sassenach*, or Saxon. The third son of Malcolm, King David I, gave great estates in Scotland to "English" Norman barons, who built castles here as they had done in England. Traces of their motte-and-bailey castles can still be detected. However, they rejected claims that they should regard themselves as vassals to the

Overleaf: Tioram Castle, Lochaber, in the Scottish Highlands, stands in a romantic setting on a rocky outcrop in Loch Moidart. Built early in the thirteenth century, the five-sided stone enclosure, with rounded angles, surrounds a great tower and other buildings that are now ruined. The enclosure walls are some 30 feet high (9.1m) and 8 feet (2.4m) thick.

Below: The ruins of the majestic fourteenth-century Tantallon Castle, built on a promontory atop sheer 100-foot (30.5m) cliffs above the Firth of Forth in Lothian, Scotland. Seen below are the remains of the gatehouse tower and barbican, built into the 50-foot (15.2m) curtain wall and projecting into a deep ditch, and two cylindrical mural towers. Bass Rock Lighthouse stands on a nearby island (below, right) as testament to the perils of these waters.

crown of England for these estates. The Scottish king (when it suited) owed allegiance to England for his many estates in England, held by his family since the time of Alfred the Great. This was not dissimilar to the feudal relationship between the kings of England and France over the former's possessions in mainland France, and resulted in similar strife. The net result of all this was that there were, in effect, two Scotlands: the English/French-speaking feudalized Lowlands and the Gaelic-speaking Celtic Highlands, which included a large Viking element and the descendants of a Lord of the Isles who professed allegiance either to the king of Scotland, the king of Norway, or to neither party.

Clearly, this explosive situation called for a king possessing strength of character and military means to impose his will on his country, as well as the diplomatic skill to avoid open confrontation with his neighbor, England. The existence of the powerful Scottish clans, the prevalent blood feuds and alliances among them and the rival claims of powerful families to a Scottish throne that had several underage sovereigns all contributed to the proliferation of castles here. There are well over a hundred of them, many with the same characteristics as their contemporaries in England. However, particular mention must be made of the two most famous castles, at Edinburgh and Stirling.

We have seen that the great castle builder Edward I of England failed to subjugate Scotland, and died in 1307 of dysentery and exhaustion attempting to do so. However, his title, "Hammer of the Scots," was not claimed by his son, Edward II, during whose reign Scottish independence was won and secured by Robert the Bruce (king of Scotland from 1306 to 1329). With his main ally, Sir James Douglas, Robert subdued all opposition, starting with the recapture of Castle Douglas near Lanark and the defeat of his major enemy, John MacDougal, in battle. After conquering his castle at Dunstaffnage, he focused on the English-held castles. In 1308 the one at Forfar was taken by escalation, and the campaign continued until 1314, when Roxburgh Castle was taken by surprise. In that same year, mighty Edinburgh castle was captured by a select band that scaled the 270-foot (82.3m) north face of the crag on which it stands. Edinburgh and Roxburgh were dismantled—that is, made ineffective—and only Stirling remained in English hands: Edward I, using the greatest collection of siege engines ever seen in Britain, had taken Stirling in 1304. Robert's brother, Edward Bruce, finally took it only after a traditional siege and the defeat of an English relief force at the Battle of Bannockburn (1314). This would be the end of the War of Independence, but armed conflict and raids from both sides of the border continued,

Above: Built by the Celts, the circular stone ring-fort at Staigue, in County Kerry, Ireland, has a diameter of some 90 feet (27.4m) and is enclosed by walls 13 feet (4.0m) thick and 18 feet (5.5m) high. Two watertight oval chambers about 7 feet (2.1m) high are built into the walls, and there are two X-shaped stairways leading to the top of the rampart. The fort was constructed of stone, without mortar, in the first century BC.

counter attempts to fire the building. There were no windows, or only extremely narrow ones, on the lower floors. Entrance was on the first floor, with the aid of a ladder that could easily be withdrawn. If there was a heavy door on the ground floor, it would often be protected by a yett, or hinged iron grill. As in other castles, a spiral staircase, known as a turnpike—either let into the wall or housed in a small, projecting wing— spiraled clockwise to give the defender above the advantage of easier use of his sword arm and maximum protection for his unguarded left side. The roof often had battlements, and small turrets at the corners allowed missiles to be dropped on an enemy seeking to force entrance. A beacon was used to summon help from neighbors, and the ground floor was used for stores. If there was room, some livestock could also be accommodated there, but normally, given warning, they would be herded into a walled or stockaded courtyard, smaller than a bailey, but sufficient to deter a casual marauder. These walled yards were called "barmkins" or "peels," giving rise to the name "peel-tower," even when the wall has disappeared.

Inevitably, larger and more sophisticated tower-houses developed. Comlongen, in Dumfries, had five stories with small chambers built into its 11-foot (3.5m) walls. Later, more living space was sometimes provided by an extra wing built on at right angles, producing an L-shaped ground plan. Indeed, some later tower-houses boasted two towers projecting from diagonally opposite corners— the so-called Z-plan. Gun loops became normal, channeled low down in the walls, but the ambitious additions of several towers and machicolations built on corbels are somewhat disapproved of by the modern purist. These tower-houses—indeed, all types of existing castles—came into their own in 1570 during a savage three-year civil war.

as they had since the English invasion of 1296. Thus a new kind of castle emerged in Scotland and the English border country. Known as tower-houses, they were well fortified to protect their owners from the robber bands, known as reivers, who plagued the lands—lightly armed enemies who could not conduct a siege.

Some 700 of these small castles were built, varying from the earliest at Drum and Crichton to the later, highly developed versions like Craigievar and Crathes. The tower-houses resembled the brochs of a much earlier era and some of the earlier Norman keeps. The first tower-houses were usually two or three times as tall as they were broad and had one chamber on each floor. The ground floor had a vaulted stone ceiling, to

There are more castles in Ireland than in England, Scotland and Wales put together. By one estimate, more than three thousand were built between 1170 and 1700, many by invaders or settlers who never became completely integrated with the Gaelic-speaking peoples. The numerous hill-forts in Ireland were constructed by the Celts who came to live there, but there is evidence that before their arrival their predecessors, stone-age peoples, lived in "crannogs," timber houses built on artificial islands in lakes. Some of these survived until medieval times. The Celts built ring-forts, often on the top of hills: good examples can be seen at Staigue, near Killarney; Dun Ogil, in the Arran Islands; and at Grianon of Aileach, in County Donegal. These should not be confused with the brochs of Scotland, although they are obviously related.

Viking invaders established the main towns in Ireland, notably Dublin, Wicklow and Waterford, which were fortified, but the first castles proper were erected by Norman invaders and settlers. In 1166, when the Irish king of Leinster was driven out of his kingdom by an alliance between a neighboring king and the "Ostmen" (Danes) of Wexford, he made the fatal mistake of appealing for help to the all-powerful English king, Henry II, who had been given papal authority over Ireland in 1155. A force was assembled from Anglo-Norman lords in southwest Wales, who were familiar with fighting Celts. Their leader was the Marcher lord Richard FitzGilbert de Clare, earl of Pembroke, known as Strongbow (who probably saw himself, being a Norman, as a future Irish king). The Celts and Danes were no match for the disciplined Anglo-Norman army—mailed mounted knights, archers and foot soldiers—and they were swiftly overcome. The plains, coastal areas and riverways were soon dominated by Anglo-Norman lords, who built the motte-and-bailey castles seen in England a century before, followed by the great stone castles we are familiar with from earlier European history. Henry II visited Ireland in 1171 with an impressive force to confirm his authority, and reserved Dublin with its hinterland, the coastal lands from Bray to Arklow, Wexford and Waterford to the English Crown. The "kingdom" of Meath, for example, was given to Hugh de Lacy to counterbalance the increasing power of Strongbow, and soon it was studded with the castles of his vassals and fellow knights.

Below: There can be few better examples of an Irish tower-house castle than Dunguaire, Kinvara, County Galway. This castle was built in the sixteenth century on the site of a ring-fort. One of the tower-house walls is integrated into the wall of the bawn, which has six sides and a small tower at one corner. The tower has four stories and an attic, with centrally placed machicolation boxes on all four sides at the level of the crenellated parapet.

Above: Castle Roche, County Louth, Ireland, was the guardian of a pass in the Armagh hills. A great stone tower-keep was built on the clifftop site of a motte-and-bailey castle in 1236, and high curtain walls were added some two decades later. Castle Roche was triangular in plan; it had a huge four-storied twin-towered gatehouse and a cylindrical tower 27 feet (8.2m) in diameter, situated in an angle. A large great hall was built inside the bailey.

Later, King John of England did an unusually good job (for him) in Ireland by consolidating his authority and organizing an active central government controlled from the newly built Dublin Castle. John took over what was probably the first stone castle to be built in Ireland, Carrickfergus, in County Antrim. The great tower, an archetypal Norman keep, was started here in 1190, and by 1200 it had been acquired as a seat of local government, remaining a possession of the British Crown until 1928. At first the network of castles in Anglo-Norman lands fostered peace and prosperity. New towns emerged around the

castles and thrived, but on the borders with the Gaelic lands there was constant unrest, almost as much as existed among the Gaelic chiefdoms. For various reasons, often England's preoccupation with internal problems, Gaelic resistance flourished, and English rule was eventually restricted to the area around Dublin called the Pale and the three great Anglo-Irish lordships, the earldoms of Ormond (Butler), Desmond and Kildare. The stone enclosure castles built during this period were of as many diverse shapes and sizes as their contemporaries in the rest of Europe, some built on the sites of hill-forts. There appeared to be a preference for massive great towers, similar to the donjons then typical of England and Normandy. Many of these castles, or their ruins, survive, notably Castle Roche in County Louth, built in the thirteenth century and now a romantic ruin.

The next significant phase of castle building in Ireland stemmed from a 1429 statute of Henry VI, which granted that any subject in the counties of Dublin, Meath, Kildare and Louth "who chooses to build a castle or tower sufficiently embattled or fortified" should be subsidized to the tune of £10. This attempt to achieve a degree of stability resulted in a plethora of castles from that period, some still known as "Ten Pound Castles." These "fortalices," or tower-houses, were well-fortified homes for wealthy men and their families rather than military strongholds. They are very similar to the Scottish tower-houses, and were built by Anglo-Norman, Anglo-Irish and Gaelic Irish alike. Many are in ruins, a fact that is often attributed to Cromwell (certainly by the Irish), but some also suffered in the war between William III and his exiled predecessor, James II.

The early years of the seventeenth century saw a new phase of castle building when Elizabeth I and the Stuarts were encouraging both English and Scottish Protestant settlers to occupy lands from which their rightful owners had been evicted. These estates were called plantations, and the castles the settlers were required to build were called plantation castles. Most of these were tower-houses, some were merely walled enclosures (bawns), and a few were rather more elaborate castles. A typical stone tower-house had walls some 6 to 8 feet (1.8 to 2.4m) thick and could be as high as six stories. The entrance was at ground level, with wooden stairs leading to the base of a stone staircase, either straight or spiral, built directly into the walls. Most had parapets that had "stepped" merlons—popular in Ireland but not unique to that country. Machicolations, often boxed or rectilinear, were provided to protect the entrances, and bartizans and turrets were functional rather than ornamental. Garderobes and fireplaces were built into the walls. The walled area around the tower-house was called a bawn, the equivalent to the Scottish peel or barmkin, and this could have circular towers at some corners. As in Scotland, the simple single tower-house evolved, and additions brought about the L-plan and Z-plan structures, that is, a tower with another adjoining at a corner, or with two towers at diagonal corners.

Below: The impressive circular tower of Doonagore Castle, with its stepped merlons, crenellated parapet and arrow loops, stands at the corner of its bawn. The 700-foot (213m) Cliffs of Moher at Doolin, on the Atlantic coast of County Clare, are almost vertical, which made this location attractive for a castle builder.

Above: Bran, in the Transylvanian Alps of Romania, is acknowledged as one of the most spectacular castles in a land noted for them. Perched on rocky crag, a timber structure was built here early in the thirteenth century, commanding the entrance to two valleys. The present medieval castle was built in 1377 to defend the city of Brasov, some 15 miles (24 km) away. It played an important part in the struggle against the Ottoman Turkish invasion of Europe in the fifteenth century.

LOOKING EASTWARD

Eastern and southeastern Europe have numerous breathtakingly beautiful castles, many of which are located in what are now Poland and Lithuania, providing evidence of the Polish/Lithuanian resistance to the Teutonic Knights. For example, the stronghold at Trakai, sited on an island in Lake Galva, some seventeen miles west of the Lithuanian capital, Vilnius, is one of the few castles in this area that was based on water defenses. Home of the duke of Lithuania in the early fifteenth century, this structure may well have been built on the site of earlier fortifications.

The Avars occupied part of Hungary until Charlemagne annihilated them in 791. He annexed all their territory, appropriated their treasure and "encouraged" the conversion of survivors to Christianity. They became absorbed into the states later founded by the Slavs and Bulgars. The raids and incursions of various warlike peoples into the lands of Charlemagne's successors initiated defensive castle building. The fierce Magyars were well to the fore in these invasions and by 955 had conquered what we now call Hungary. They, in turn, were defeated at the Battle of Lechfeld by the renowned Holy Roman Emperor Otto I.

Their ruler became a Christian, and in 1001 his son, Stephen I, was recognized as king by the pope. The following centuries saw the familiar struggles for power between noble families, civil wars and expansion into what is now known as the Balkans. At one point a Byzantine emperor occupied the Hungarian throne and accelerated the practice of castle building by granting lands to noble families. The Byzantines did not stay for long, but the feudalism they had fostered remained. It was just as well, however, that Hungary was now well protected by castles; it was to become a European bulwark against a great threat: the Mongols.

Under Genghis Khan, a united horde of Turkish and Mongolian tribes spread first in a wide band across northern China. Then, in 1220–21, they turned westward. Their warriors were expert horsemen and archers, and in open country, well suited to their mobile tactics, they carried all before them. They sacked Kiev in 1240 and thrust west into Poland and Hungary, destroying Krakow. In 1241–42 what was called the "Golden Horde" split in two, the northern division thrusting into Poland, where they faced an army of heavily armored mounted men-at-arms, including Teutonic Knights. This force was annihilated at the Battle of Liegnitz. The southern division, moving up the Danube, meted out a similar fate to a Hungarian army on the River Sajo. Europe was spared further devastation by disputes about succession among Genghis' heirs upon his death and internal problems among the numerous Mongolian tribes. However, these invasions showed that the mounted hordes were unable to overrun hilly country defended by castles. Their many horses needed vast tracts of grassland for fodder, and the invaders lacked the experience and equipment to take castles by storm. The castle at Salgo, some 74 miles (119.1 km) northeast of Budapest, was originally built to counter these invasions. It stands on a rock 187 feet (57m) high and has an extremely powerful keep. At Sárospatak, on the border with today's Slovakia, a twelfth-century castle was considerably strengthened to repel the Mongols. After their invasions withered away, Hungary was rebuilt, and the power of its nobles waxed and waned under successive rulers.

In 1308 the Angevin noble Charles I came to power, and Hungary's rule expanded into Bosnia and what is now Serbia. It became one of Europe's most prosperous countries, incorporating many smaller vassal states to the southeast. However, another major threat was developing, as the successors to the "Golden Horde," the Ottoman Empire, gathered both strength and impetus. Leaving Constantinople behind them, an isolated Byzantine island, the Ottomans conquered and occupied those Balkan states that had acted as a buffer between the Muslim and Christian worlds. In 1389 a Serb-led alliance to repulse the Ottomans was crushed at Kosovo, and in 1396 the army of King Sigismund of Hungary was annihilated in a similar attempt. The declining importance of the castle was underscored by a strong religious movement that arose in Hungary, its militancy rooted in the excommunication and execution of Jan Hus in 1415. A preacher at the University of Prague, Hus was a forerunner of the Reformation, challenging the infallibility of the pope and advocating the Bible as the supreme Christian authority. Worse still, he had criticized the Church for the sale of indulgences. His followers continued to propagate these heretical views and became involved in politics, endangering Sigismund's claim to the throne of Bohemia. A Crusade against the Hussites (as they were called) was declared, and a series of battles was fought (1419–36) between Imperial forces and the competent and well-led Hussites. Eventually, internal ideological struggles weakened the movement, and the Crusade was all but over by 1434. However, although the Hussites hated castles as symbols of oppression, their great leader Jan Zizka turned the hill town of Tabor, their "Holy City" south of Prague, into a stronghold. The Hussites built the castle of Kalich so their leader could use the name Jan of Kalich (Chalice), symbolizing their belief that communion should be taken as both bread and wine. The castle is still to be seen in Bohemia, now in the Czech Republic. Space does not permit a detailed study of their military tactics, but their use of armored wagons as movable and effective castles (*Wagenburg*), stoutly defended by infantry using hand guns, and light field artillery, was another reason for the decline of castle-dominated warfare.

The Turkish campaign to overrun Europe continued in fits and starts, and another crushing defeat of Hungarian-led forces at Kosovo in 1448 consolidated Ottoman gains. However, a watershed in our story was the capture of Constantinople in 1453. The famous walls finally succumbed to the use of "a mighty bombard" so huge that it had to be cast on site. The siege cannon had arrived! The Ottoman advances continued, and the Hungarians met an army comprising exceptionally well-disciplined and fanatical infantry—the Janissaries, bodyguards of the Sultan; heavy and light cavalry; increasingly efficient artillery; engineers; and miners. Against this force, the Hungarians had a chain of some fifty-five castles scattered irregularly along their border, but these seemed inadequate to provide an effective defense. One historian (Hans Zinsser, author of *Rats, Lice and History*), reports that these castles "were without organization, fighting as much with one another as with the Turks." He also introduces yet another significant reason for the decline in importance of castles in warfare—disease. In 1456 the Ottoman siege of

Belgrade was relieved because the Turks were incapacitated by disease—possibly the first appearance of typhus in this region. An Imperial army was defeated in 1542 before it had a chance to engage the Turks when some 30,000 men died in a typhus epidemic. In 1566 the Emperor Maximilian II had to abandon an advance against the Ottoman position when his army was smitten with typhus and his troops deserted, thus spreading the disease throughout Europe. The threat of typhus, a "new" disease, militated against embarking on a long, static siege with a large army. Eventually, after a Hungarian army was roundly defeated at the Battle of Mohács in 1526, and Louis II, king of Hungary and Bohemia, fell, Hungary was divided between the Ottoman Empire and an emerging Austria. Ottoman advances were finally checked at Vienna in 1529, Malta in 1565 and Lepanto in 1571, after which their conquering and expanding empire stagnated. However, they had proved that the traditional tactics of a feudal army and its dependence on medieval castles had become ineffective in the face of a modern army equipped with cannon.

Radical changes in castle design appeared first in Bohemia, as a result of its experience with the successful Ottoman attacks. The principal line of defense was transferred to the outer wall, reinforced by massive bastion towers, some of which were pointed in the direction of the enemy, and barbicans fitted with gun ports were the norm. The constant threat of Turkish invasion stimulated a program of new castle building and restructuring throughout Austria, Hungary, Germany and other central and eastern European lands.

Experts claim that the bastion system of defense, soon to be adopted throughout Europe, originated in Bohemia. Existing castles were also modified to house artillery, towers being strengthened and shortened to

Left. The aptly named "Swallow's Nest" castle in Yalta, the Ukraine, is perched high above the Black Sea on a perpendicular crag that protects it on the three seaward sides. By 1481 the Ottoman Turks had occupied the Crimea, and the Black Sea became the "Ottoman Lake." The Crimean Tartars became the slave-runners of southern Russia, exporting thousands of captives every year as the spoils of their forays into Poland and the Ukraine. Russian forces captured the Crimea in 1774, and many thousands of Tartars fled west of the Black Sea.

withstand the tremendous recoil of a heavy gun. Some towers designed specifically for the mounting of cannon were introduced, and walls were made more resistant to the shock of cannon-fire by piling up rammed earth behind them. An artillery duel between besieger and defender was not unusual, and the use of mortars to lob heavy missiles over the highest walls must have had a considerable effect on morale. Even as late as the English Civil War (1642–49) many existing castles played a role, some holding out for quite long periods against besieging forces. Corfe Castle, for example, withstood heavy Puritan bombardment for nine months.

THE RISE OF THE ARTILLERY FORT

In the history of fortification, the end of the era of the castle, the fortified home of a medieval lord, overlapped its successor, the artillery fort. Wars in Europe were as common and devastating as they had been in the Middle Ages. The rivalry between Hapsburg and Valois, the Thirty Years' War, Louis XIV's wars of expansion, the Wars of Spanish succession, the Seven Years' War, to name but a few of the major conflicts, all contributed to advances in military tactics, weaponry and defenses. However, because of the changes in attack weaponry, the artillery fortress became the focus of fortification design.

Right: Deal Castle was one of several artillery fortresses built by Henry VIII to protect the south coast of England from anticipated invasions by the French in 1538–39. The stone-lined moat, 50 feet (15.2m) wide and 16 feet (4.9m) deep, was covered by fifty-four handgun embrasures set in the base of the outer bastions. The flat roofs of the six semicircular bastions, which project from a circular central building, are the platforms for the fort's main artillery. The central building, a form of keep, has, in turn, six inner semicircular bastions with flat roofs, whose parapets are slightly higher than the outer bastions. These are also gun platforms and have loops for handguns. The flat roof of the keep acts as a third level of gun platform. The fortress has a single entrance, equipped with murder-holes, approached by a stone causeway with a drawbridge. The location of the fortress below ground level helped protect the fortress against the broadsides of passing battleships.

Leaders in the field of fortress design were the Italian family of Sangallos, whose services were soon in demand throughout Europe, in direct proportion to the proliferation of portable cannon. To quote John Keegan, "The bastion fortress restored the advantage of defence over offence as rapidly as cannon had reversed it at the end of the fifteenth century. By the end of the sixteenth, the frontiers of every state that aspired to preserve its sovereignty were protected at the most vulnerable points—mountain passes, river crossings, navigable estuaries—by modern defences."

Henry VIII of England (1509–47) saw the writing on the wall when, by opting out of the Roman Church, he made an enemy of the Pope. Having robbed the rich monasteries he had dissolved, Henry invested the money in the construction of over twenty massive artillery forts on the south coast of England with a completely new design, as well as modifying and modernizing existing castles to receive and deliver artillery fire. A single large warship of those days could carry as many heavy cannon as an army, and could easily bombard and destroy conventional coastal defenses while cruising by, so the aim was to lower as much as possible of the structure to below ground level.

A good example of an early artillery fortress is at Deal, on the coast of Kent. This had a round central "keep" (for want of a better word), with six slightly lower semicircular bastions radiating from it. A lower "curtain wall" surrounds this, which also consists of six semicircular bastions. A deep surrounding dry moat, covered by gun ports, is enclosed by a six-lobed outermost wall. The roofs of all the bastions and the keep were strong enough to carry the heaviest guns, so in effect three tiers of heavy cannon could be brought to bear on an attacking enemy. Some fifty-four loops for

handguns were set in the curtain-wall bastions covering the moat, while thirty loops covered the "bailey." The latest cannon were mounted on wheeled carriages, easily moved to adjoining bastions to provide concentrated fire. It is not known why Henry did not use the more common sharply pointed bastion, although later English fortresses

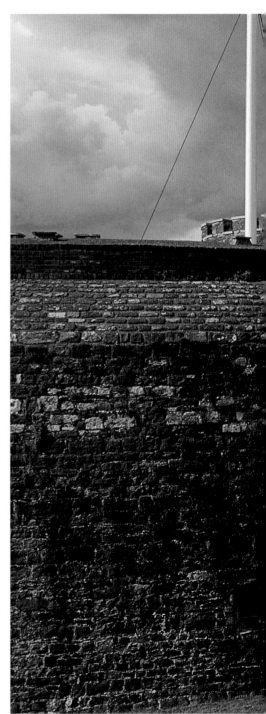

certainly did. The later developments provided a succession of pointed bastions protecting each other, thus replacing the height of the castle with depth, keeping the enemy at a distance, each successive bastion being also an artillery platform, all forming a star-shaped ground plan. A sophisticated approach was developed by the besieger, involving digging saps and parallel trenches, protected batteries being pushed ever nearer, and undermining. Many of these later, huge, fortresses are still to be seen in the Low Countries, and for the castle aficionado, the key name to be dropped here is Vauban, the justifiably famous seventeenth-century French military engineer.

INSIDE THE
CASTLE WALLS

We have yet to see (or surmise) what everyday life in a castle was like. This question is not easy to answer: although we can examine the remains of a castle—even its ruins—traces of how the occupants lived have long since disappeared. The archaeologist can provide only limited assistance here, and the historian has to rely on contemporary literature and original sources, including manor rolls, bills and court cases. Further, we must take an overview of the same long period on which we based our study of castle design. This entails wide generalization over diverse cultures and several centuries.

As "the fortified residence of a lord," in broad definition, castles housed several types of occupants. Monarchs and great nobles possessed many castles, some of which are better described as fortified palaces. John of Gaunt, the younger son of Edward III of England, was married by his father to the heiress of the duke of Lancaster, and on her father's death succeeded to the title and more than thirty castles. When not engaged in warfare, noblemen would visit all these in turn with their huge retinues, if only to consume the year's worth of food that their bailiffs had stored for them and hunt their forests for the game that had been preserved for their pleasure. Perhaps more representative is the lesser noble—a member of the "second estate" that developed in Europe. The first estate was the Church, and the third comprised, roughly, the rest of the population—the serfs, villeins and craftsmen on whom the estate's economy depended. Major towns, of course, would also have at least one castle, often built by the magnate on whose lands they stood. Many financial advantages accrued from controlling the town's inhabitants and, by licence, its markets, which were a steady source of income.

There can be little doubt that life in a newly constructed motte-and-bailey castle, or in a narrow Bergfried, was extremely uncomfortable for all who lived there. As we have seen, the knights who ventured out on land-grabbing adventures were recruited because they had little wealth of their own: they sought riches and status by plunder, ransom and by wringing an income from new lands granted by their leader. But as time went by, a family could accumulate wealth by wise husbandry, "suitable" marriages and, for the successful warrior, large ransoms. The entire estate, called a "manor" in England, existed to put money into the owner's pocket, at the expense of the peasantry it was supposed to protect. Of course, there were expenses, including the demands made by the occupant's feudal superior. The accouterments essential to knightly status— armor and war horse alone—were extremely expensive. In many cases, a young man suited by birth and upbringing for knighthood could not afford them. On the other hand, in many countries some of the great nobles were wealthier than their sovereigns, and used this fact for leverage. An analysis of the number of nobles, knights and "gentry" in England in 1436 suggests that about one thousand belonged to the baronial class, (members of the peerage and their families) and 5,000 to the knightly class, with their families. Some 5,000 were squires and 22,000 were considered gentry, amounting to 1.7 percent of the population. (Gentry included clerics of several degrees, civil servants, administrators of various kinds and clerks, many of whom also held a minor priestly office, like deacon, having attended a university. Thomas á Becket, chancellor of England and archbishop of Canterbury, was the son of a London trader. He earned a degree at the University of Paris and started his career as a clerk in London.

Previous pages: Bamburgh Castle stands on a 150-foot (45.7m) cliff headland on England's North Sea coast on the site of Iron Age and Roman fortifications. Bamburgh derives from Bebbanburh (Bebba's Town), named for the Saxon Queen Bebba. The castle withstood an attack by the Danes in the ninth century; the first Norman castle here was besieged in 1095, and it remained a royal castle until the seventeenth century. The 65-foot (19.8m) donjon-keep, dating from about 1160–70, is typical of those of Henry II. During the Wars of the Roses the Yorkists besieged the castle twice: the latter attack, in 1464, was the first time in England's history that artillery brought down a castle's walls.

Chaucer gives a very good summary of the economies of a castle in his description of the reeve (originally a representative of the peasants who served alongside the bailiff, the knight's administrator). Over time, his role became much more important:

He kept his bins and garners very trim;
No auditor could gain a point on him.
And he could judge by watching
*   drought and rain*
The yield he might expect from seed and grain.
His master's sheep, his animals and hens,
Pigs, horses, dairies, stores and cattle-pens
Were wholly trusted to his government.

In this list of the farm produce from the castle's lands, sheep were the "cash crop." English wool was of excellent quality and highly prized by Continental weavers, especially in Flanders. A knight in Gascony would earn a very fair income from his vineyards. And local lords who had control of a pass, river ford, or bridge in their diverse regions gained income by imposing tolls. The knight depended on his bailiff and reeve to squeeze the last groat out of every peasant in his manor, or manors. Besides working for nothing on his lord's fields, the peasant often had to pay to grind his own corn in the lord's mill and even to bake his bread in the lord's oven. There were many degrees of peasantry, from the lowly serf to the yeoman, with varying duties, taxes and privileges. Taxes included a form of inheritance tax when a son took over his deceased father's fields, and payment when a daughter married away from the manor. Only in the wake of the Black Death did all this begin to change, as the peasant became aware of his growing importance in the agricultural economy. Then the manor, which had

Above: The Alhambra (Arabic for the "Red One") in Granada, Spain, is one of the wonders of the medieval world. Within its walls are courtyards featuring fountains, pools and luscious vegetation—the ultimate luxury for a people of desert origins.

Above: A view inside the ruins of the extensive domestic buildings raised in the 1370s by John of Gaunt (younger son of Edward III of England) in Kenilworth Castle. A later owner, Robert Dudley, Earl of Leicester, added a further range of domestic buildings. Note the fireplaces and grand windows, which are typical of Tudor architecture.

not find a niche to sleep in elsewhere—as, for example, the cook in the kitchen. It was also used as the manor court and, of course, for feasts and banquets. The knight and his family usually had a private sleeping area at the end of the hall, called the solar, while retainers slept on the floor on pallets filled with straw. The floor was covered with rushes, frequently renewed, since unwanted food was thrown down for the dogs. Boards laid on trestles served as tables, with a "cup board"—another trestle table—at the side for serving. The knight, his family and their guests sat at the head, on a dais. After the great hall was built as a separate structure in the inner bailey, then incorporated into the structure of the concentric and rectangular castle, a suite of rooms became available for the lord and his family. Living accommodations could be located in multistory towers, and a guest might share his chamber with a cannon. In a royal castle, the constable would have his living quarters in the gatehouse. The pervasive threat of attack was attested by the bows, sheaves of arrows, bills and pikes stored at the arrow loops and entrances, which gave rise to the Victorians' display of weapons on the walls of Gothic-style houses.

A large castle had to accommodate its garrison and the knights called up for expected service in times of war. These spaces might be closed down or put to other uses in peacetime, as the permanent staff of a modest castle could be quite small. Many nobles took in the sons of knights, not necessarily their own vassals, for training in the only career open to them, the profession of arms. They were drilled regularly in weaponry and riding skills.

Because of the risk of fire, the wooden kitchen was usually apart from the living quarters. Later, the use of stone or brick construction moved it closer to, or inside, the main building. The kitchen included

been virtually self-sufficient, became increasingly expensive, as the need for greater comfort and sophistication—a higher standard of living as we would call it—evolved. The ostentatious display of wealth became important in the social life of the Middle Ages, with the need to provide lavish hospitality for an influential guest.

When the castle era began, the great hall served as both eating and sleeping accommodations for almost everyone who could the buttery, which was the storeroom for liquor and gave us the term "butler," and the pantry was used to store the other provisions. The peasants lived mainly on a gruel or flat pancake made from some coarse grain, or from peas or beans. Castle dwellers had bread made of flour ground from wheat. Brown bread made from rye flour was also a staple food. The Church forbade red meat for three days a week (later, only Fridays) and throughout Lent, so every castle (and monastery) had its fishpond stocked with carp; eel was also a favorite dish. Fish could be preserved in salt, or smoked, in the absence of refrigeration.

Sheep and cows' milk were used to make butter and cheese: heavily salted, they kept for long periods. The nursery rhyme tells us that curds and whey were not wasted, and chickens and ducks provided a plentiful supply of eggs and poultry. Most birds were regarded as edible, including swans, cranes, blackbirds and larks. (One wonders how many larks it took to make a gourmet dish of larks' tongues.) Most castles had a dovecote in the bailey, and rabbits were guarded by the warrener. Deer and wild boar were hunted for food and protected from poaching by rigorous game laws. The usual methods of cooking were roasting, boiling and stewing. Meat pies and pasties were also popular. (Frying was unusual, since animal fat was a valuable commodity needed for soap, candles and lubricants.) Whole oxen were roasted on spits for major feasts; smaller spits were often turned by dogs harnessed to a gear mechanism.

Honey from the castle's beehives was used for sweetening. Expensive spices from the East, made known through the Crusades, were kept under lock and key. Vegetables grown in kitchen gardens included cabbages, turnips, lettuces, pumpkins, cucumbers, leeks, onions, peas and beans. Garlic,

mint, thyme, fennel, parsley and other herbs still in use were cultivated to add savor. Most estates had an orchard for the production of various fruits and berries: apples, pears, plums and cherries were cooked in pastries and served with cream. Vineyards were uncommon in the north, where wine had to be imported from Spain, Germany and France. Brewhouses produced ale and mead for the castle's staff.

Below: These massive twelfth-century Norman archways in Kenilworth Castle contrast strikingly with the sophisticated fourteenth- and fifteenth-century architecture shown in the illustration opposite.

Above: *Schloss Burg, a large medieval castle on the River Wupper in the Bergisches Land, northern Germany, was extensively rebuilt at the turn of the nineteenth and twentieth centuries. The castle now houses the Bergisches Museum, which displays the history and culture of those living within its walls through the ages. This display shows a living room as it may have been in the late Middle Ages.*

Water supply, an essential, was usually from a well. When no well was available, as often happened in the Crusader states, huge cisterns were dug to hold rainwater, and spring water from the hills was carried by aqueducts.

Table manners evolved to display one's good breeding. Plates and personal cutlery were unknown, but the rich had silver spoons; knives and bowls were shared. Sticking one's little finger out when drinking, still practiced by some today, is an amusing relic. Chaucer, tongue in cheek, gives us an insight in his famous description of the Nun in *The Canterbury Tales*:

> *At meat her manners were well-taught withal;*
> *No morsel from her lips did she let fall,*
> *Nor dipped her fingers in the sauce too deep;*
> *But she could carry a morsel up and keep*
> *The smallest drop from falling on her breast.*

Before a meal, servants poured water over the company's hands and cut loaves of bread into thick slices to serve as plates. Guests who sat with their host on the dais received the top of the first loaf—"upper crust"—and they sat "above the salt" [container]. Great feasts figured in the diplomacy of the age, honoring such occasions as a dynastic marriage, or visits from another sovereign.

To the modern eye, castle furnishings would seem very sparse. Only the lord and his family had beds—leather thongs strung on a frame, with a feather mattress, bed linen and colorful woollen or fur coverlets. Beds also served as seats, and were often located near the fireplaces that became increasingly common in private apartments. Bed curtains either hung from the ceiling or from rails attached to the four corner posts with a canopy across the top. They helped to keep drafts out and provided some privacy. Guests were provided with beds, but they were expected to bring their own bed linen. No one slept alone: the single bed belonged to a later age.

Chairs, originally scarce, increased in size and comfort, and many were collapsible for packing in the baggage train of the knight. The bare stone walls of the earlier castles were later covered with tapestries, some of rare beauty, depicting mythical and historic scenes. They also helped to insulate against the cold, drafts and damp. The major European manufacturer of tapestries was the town of Arras in Artois: not many competitors reached their high standards, and Arras tapestries became family heirlooms. In 1474 Louis XI of France destroyed Arras, and the tapestry weavers were dispersed to take up their trade in other Flemish cities; some also settled in England, Spain and Italy. Eastern rugs, wainscoting and paneling became more common, as did plastering. These amenities contributed to the comfort and beauty of castle's living quarters.

Clothing played an important role in proclaiming one's status and wealth, and was subject to the variations of fashion. In the castle's early days, even clothing for the lord and his family was comparatively modest: a simple tunic, made of wool, augmented in cold climates by a fur-lined cloak. However, contact with the exotic East resulted in new textiles including cotton, muslin (a corruption of Muslim), damask from Damascus, gauze from Gaza, baldachin from Baghdad and expensive silks from China were used to make ever-more-elaborate clothing for noblemen and -women. Both sexes began to wear long gowns of simple design, and garments were

Below: *This massive open fireplace in the pantry of Raglan Castle, Gwent, Wales, is built into a wall almost 10 feet (3.0m) thick. Fed with large logs, the fire would have been equipped with hooks for suspending cauldrons, and a huge spit would have been turned in front. Later fireplaces would have been decorated with heraldic decorations reflecting the owner's ancestry.*

Above: Gleninagh Castle, County Clare, Ireland, an L-plan tower house of the sixteenth century, was occupied until the 1800s. It was four stories high—hard work for the servants who had to get water from this well. No castle, even a comparatively modest tower-house, could survive without a reliable, defended water supply.

tailored to fit more closely, with necklines wider for women and shorter tunics for men. Closer fit demanded long buttoned openings down the front or back, and from wrist to elbow, fastened with rows of closely set buttons made of silver gilt, precious stones, or enamel, depending on the means of the wearer. Garments were parti-colored, and graced with jagged edges and patterns. Embroidery with gold and silver thread and precious stones became increasingly common for those who could afford it.

Ladies covered their hair with a wimple, and the conical and horned head coverings typical of the Middle Ages appeared in the 1420s. Men's shoes became so long and pointed that they had to be chained up to the knee and were finally restricted in length by law. The importance that was attached to upholding sharp dividing lines between the classes is reflected in laws that restricted apparel of certain materials to

the nobility; even merchants, who could afford the noble's many-colored garments with luxurious trim, had to wear long dark robes. Servants wore their master's livery, and were entitled to a new set every year. Expensive clothes were stored in a wardrobe —originally a narrow chamber for storing cloth, later a large room with its own staff to maintain the garments.

Every castle had its complement of tradesmen, craftsmen and other servants. An armorer, with a smith to assist, maintained armor and weaponry. The smith's main task was to shoe the many horses used as mounts and as draft animals for the farm. Farriers and grooms cared for them, except for the war horses that were kept on a nearby stud farm. Carpenters and masons carried out castle maintenance and improvements, while the women made woollen cloth that clothed the humbler folk, in addition to their other household tasks.

Sanitation was provided for, despite primitive knowledge of hygiene. Most rooms had chamber pots that were emptied daily. A lord and his family often had a bath in their private quarters; if not, in an area screened off near the kitchen, where water was heated in a large copper cauldron. The bathtub was rather like a large barrel, made by the castle's cooper. Soap was originally made from tallow and beech ash; later, olive oil imported from southern Europe was incorporated into it. Shaving was done with razors of various shapes, and small shears, rather like sheep shears, were used to cut hair and beards. Mirrors were made of polished steel or brass until glass mirrors made in Germany became available—at great expense. Perfumes from various sources, including flowers and musk, were treasured not only for their fragrance, but because they warded off disease.

Decoration has largely disappeared over time but we know from contemporary paintings that castle exteriors were whitewashed. The interiors were often covered in colorful painting, as were medieval churches and cathedrals. In the age of heraldry, coats of arms graced gates and the great fireplaces that became the norm. The village church housed the tombs in which the knight and his family were buried. Many were crowned with an effigy of the deceased and decorated with the family's arms. Most castles had at least one chapel, with the chaplain serving as confessor for the household and possibly as teacher for the children. Close relationships between the castle and the local monastery were the norm, with mutual benefits obtained by bartering food and services.

What did castle dwellers do for recreation? If the knight and his wife were literate,

Below: Probably more people visit Bran Castle because of its infamous former owner than for its museum of medieval art. Bran is the most spectacular castle in Romania, positioned on a precipitous crag 15 miles (24 km) southwest of Brasov in the Transylvanian Alps (exterior view, page 154). Constructed in 1377, its fifteenth-century inhabitant Vlad Tepes, better known as Vlad the Impaler, was the model for Bram Stoker's Dracula.

Above: *Heraldry played a very important role in the Middle Ages, when few could read. These arms decorate the Palace of the Grand Master of the Hospitallers on the island of Rhodes, Greece. At top center are the arms of the King of France, charged with three* fleurs de lys *and surmounted by a crown. On the left are the arms of the order.*

books (actually manuscripts) were rare and almost exclusively devotional and religious in content. Chess was played, and evidence suggests that a form of backgammon was in use. Music and poetry were very popular, and itinerant poets were welcome guests. In southern France, they were known as troubadors; in Germany, as *Minnesingers*, the most famous being Walther von der Vogelweide (around 1200). He composed in German rather than in Latin, and his lyrics often celebrated both courtly and physical love. The troubadors, who were often of noble lineage themselves, also composed in the vernacular *langue d'oc*, but rarely performed. The northern French *trouvères* composed in their vernacular, called *langue d'oil*. Minstrels, or *jongleurs*, traveled the countryside entertaining and were sometimes permanent members of a noble household. Those who could afford to also maintained troupes of actors. Some well-born women played the lute and sang to the accompaniment of the tabor (tambourine) and the stringed cithara, or zither. The role of the joker or jester is familiar to most of us.

As courtly love played an important part in upper-class medieval social life, it deserves a closer look. Strict social constraints resulted in a highly idealized form of romance, in which the "lover" offered complete devotion to his lady. As the troubadors and most of the romantic literature make clear, the object of this unbounded love was unattainable. The convention centered on the passion between a young knight and the wife of a lord who had made the customary arranged marriage. It reflected the feudal system: the lover was the "vassal" of his beloved and was subject to her will. He would suffer any hardship and risk life and limb to satisfy her slightest whim. Aware of his devotion, she encouraged it covertly. In essence, courtly love was adulterous, secretive and most importantly, always remained unconsummated.

Courtly love was part of the code of conduct known as chivalry—a rigorous system of morals and ethics whereby the Church and state sought to channel the excesses of the early Middle Ages when knights were little better than brutal armed robbers. As the feudal system evolved, a young man was dubbed a knight in a moving religious ritual, in which he swore to protect the weak, the oppressed, widows and children, and his social inferiors. Of course, this form of social control was often honored in the breach then in observance, human nature having changed little through the course of history. However, it did establish positive sanctions for altruism and undoubtedly served to set a higher standard of conduct for the powerful vis-a-vis the powerless.

The most prevalent image of the medieval castle today is that of a sunlit scene filled with tournaments and jousting, followed eagerly by fine ladies in jewels and steeple hats from gaily bedecked stands shaded by striped canopies, who cheer on the knights wearing their tokens. We have Hollywood to thank for this, although it does point up the fact that in a military culture, courage, skill at arms, horsemanship and endurance were the primary virtues. It is believed that tournaments originated in the early days in France as a means of training a troop of knights in the main tactic of battle, the cavalry charge. This evolved into the *mêlée*, a sport wherein two groups of mounted knights, often led by a senior noble, fought each other with every form of weaponry allowed—usually lance, sword and mace or battle ax. This exercise was carried out in the space between two towns or castles. The aim was to capture and ransom one's opponents, not to kill them, although, of course, both injuries and fatalities were common. Tournaments offered a prime opportunity

for the knight who sought employment to show off his abilities—a form of audition, as well as an exercise in bonding. This form of tournament became rarer as the Middle Ages progressed, evolving into the more lavish spectacles, staged to celebrate coronations, weddings and christenings.

Similarly, jousting—two knights riding against each other with couched lances, with the aim of unhorsing the opponent or splintering a lance—started as a training exercise and then became ritualized, with strict rules and a referee. Colorful descriptions in the

Above and below: Stained glass at Schloss Burg, dating from its nineteenth-century restoration. The window above probably owes more to William Morris than the medieval glass masters at Chartres, but the arms of the nearby town of Ratingen, below, are not anachronistic, having been in use since 1430.

Right: This colorful scene is from the medieval illuminated manuscript Les Très Riches Heures du Duc de Berry. *It shows a May pageant celebrated by the nobles and their ladies, with sumptuous attire made from precious materials and decorated with fur and jewels. Note the lady in the foreground, who is wearing the classic "horned" headdress.*

literature of the time were epitomized in *Tales of Arthur*, a highly romanticized version of a Celtic myth transposed into the Middle Ages. However, Arthur's knights did not favor the blunted lances that became common in later tournaments and jousts, and in Camelot, Lancelot's love *was* requited! As methods of warfare changed, and the traditional knightly role as heavy cavalry declined, the tournaments and jousts became increasingly stylized, and the armor manufactured for them became more ostentatious and cumbersome—wholly unsuitable for actual combat.

The lady of the castle, or chatelaine, when not of the highest nobility, had complete charge of running the household, and her education was directed to this end. She lived in her own separate accommodation, removed from the hubbub of daily life, where she could attend her (many) children and see that her daughters were properly brought up, her sons having been sent off to another household for education. Although some wives did accompany their husbands on campaigns and Crusades, most were left in charge of the castle during their frequent absences. Many tales attest to staunch defenses against attacks and sieges by chatelaines and their ladies. Joan of Kent, for example, the nineteen-year-old wife of the earl of Salisbury and cousin to Edward III, remained in England when her husband accompanied his sovereign to France at the start of the Hundred Years' War. In 1346 the Scots, taking advantage of the supposed absence of all defensive forces, invaded England. Before the battle of Neville's Cross, in which the Scots were soundly beaten, Joan went from battalion to battalion "desiring them to do their devoir [duty] to defend the honour of her lord the king of England and, in the name of God, every man to be of good heart and courage" (Froissart). The fact that she was reportedly the loveliest woman in England may have had something to do with the ensuing victory. It was her garter, dropped when dancing with the king at the siege of Calais,

that he used to symbolize his famous Order of the Garter, with its mysterious motto "*Honi soit qui mal y pense*"(Evil be to him who evil thinks). Joan has gone down in history as the Fair Maid of Kent, and the epitome of the proactive medieval woman (three husbands, including the last, the Black Prince) and mother of seven (including Richard II of England). In those histories that focus on kings, battles, popes, devious politics and fearful brutality, such heroines are often overlooked, but they made significant contributions to what is remembered chiefly as a fighting man's world.

Left: Another illustration from Les Très Riches Heures, *showing a betrothal in front of the castle and village of Dourdan. The book of hours was prepared in Bourges by three Dutch manuscript illuminators, the brothers Limbourg, in the late fourteenth century.*

Schloss Burg

North-Rhein Westphalia, Germany

Schloss Burg, guarding the River Wupper in North-Rhein Westphalia, Germany, was noted in medieval times for its *Schildmauer*, a very high curtain wall between towers or crags to protect the side of the castle. Some accommodation was provided by overhanging, half-timbered constructions (*Holzriegalbau* or *Fachwerksbau*), on internal galleried corridors overlooking the courtyards as seen in the view opposite. When Schloss Burg was extensively rebuilt, around 1903, to form a restaurant, this half-timbering was carefully reproduced, and many medieval-style wall paintings were used to decorate the *Rittersaal* or *Palas*, the main living accommodation. While the restoration was not entirely historically accurate, the castle is now a well-maintained building that provides a better idea of castle life during the Middle Ages than could be found at a ruin. The castle is now a museum, the Bergisches Museum, where displays focus on life in the Bergischen Land during the Middle Ages and later.

Above: An interesting mixture of styles is evident in this comfortable living room. The baby's crib and spinning wheel could well have belonged in a medieval castle.

Below: In the Middle Ages every castle had a chapel, and most had a chaplain, who might also act as teacher and advisor. The quality of the statues and frescoes would reflect the wealth and status of the castle's owner.

Below: This pharmacy is considerably more sophisticated than its predecessor from the Middle Ages. It dates from the mid-1800s, when medicine was making great advances.

THE END
OF IT ALL

The need for the castle as fortified residence waned when the feudal system gave place to strong central governments. They defended their state boundaries with artillery fortresses, and the town and family castles of the Middle Ages were either retained by their owners as prestigious symbols, or allowed to fall into ruin. In the former case, noble families prided themselves on the fact that their forebears had built "their" castles, even when they had, in reality, been the gift of a monarch to a favorite. This tendency to romanticize may help explain why the medieval castle is still so widely considered a thing of beauty, irrespective of its actual aesthetic. No one would claim that the motte-and-bailey castle was beautiful, but its immediate successors acquired this elusive quality in the popular mind. Those built later, during the fourteenth and fifteenth centuries, were often, in fact, exceptionally handsome.

A case in point is Bodiam Castle, built in 1386 in the county of Sussex, near England's south coast. It is a fine example of the rectangular courtyard layout, set in a moat wide enough to be a small lake. Bodiam could serve as a model for the ideal castle, with drum towers at each corner, an impressive front gatehouse and rear postern, and rectangular mural towers set into both of the side curtain walls. The living space, housed entirely in the two-story integral accommodation, is adorned with crenellations, machicolations and gun and arrow loops. It had a strategic role, as it would have hindered a French army seeking to invade the hinterland, but one senses that the owner's primary aim was to impress his peers with his stately home. This trend would result in the fortified manors that eventually replaced the castle in Europe— until the advent of the "pseudo-castle"

described later. Sir Edward Dalyngrygge, one of Edward III's successful generals, built the castle at Bodiam, which is now visited by thousands each year. It was carefully restored in the 1920s by Lord Curzon, who reported that he had counted thirty-three fireplaces and twenty-four lavatories, all with drainage built into the walls.

Roger de Fiennes, who was treasurer of the royal household, built himself a superb castle not far from Bodiam: Henry VI granted his license to crenellate in 1441, and his master-builder produced what must have been a magnificently comfortable home. Herstmonceux, also in Sussex, is rectangular, built of brick and surrounded by a wide moat. It has octagonal and semioctagonal towers, and a most imposing gatehouse complete with arrow and gun loops, machicolations, turrets and a double fighting platform. Peeping over the high curtain walls, one can see the tiled rooftops of the sumptuous two-story integrated dwelling. The well-known historian Paul Johnson refers accurately to this type of castle as a "castle-mansion."

Gratitude is due to those individuals who have used their wealth to restore historic castles faithfully and convert them to magnificent modern residences. They include several members of the remaining European royalty, other noble families and a number of wealthy Americans. Leeds Castle, in Kent, was purchased by the Hon. Olive Lady Baillie, an Anglo-American, in 1926 and restored with "meticulous care" as a living history book, rather than a stone museum. The barbican and constable's accommodations date to the late Middle Ages, and the Tudor monarch Henry VIII (1491–1574) enlarged the castle's residence. The American connection came through Sir John Culpeper, a loyal servant of the Crown, who was granted more than five

Previous pages: The Château de Chambord, overlooking the River Cosson in the Loire Valley, France, is a truly magnificent spectacle. A symbol of wealth and power, the building demonstrates that the need for a strongly fortified, siege-resistant dwelling had passed when this Renaissance retreat was constructed on the site of a medieval castle in 1515. Chambord would be more accurately termed a palais *than a* château: *the great drum towers and the machicolations above the entrance are more architectural whimsy than fortification. It has been suggested that Leonardo da Vinci may have been involved in the design, since he was invited by François I to live at nearby Amboise in his old age.*

million acres in the colony of Virginia. He had also inherited Leeds Castle, which passed to his daughter and heiress, who married the fifth Lord Fairfax. A descendent of the Fairfax family sold its American estates in 1806 and invested much of the proceeds in restoring the Leeds castle complex to the medieval style. It now belongs to the British nation and is a popular tourist venue and conference center. At one point *another* rich American was interested in buying Leeds Castle. The legendary newspaper tycoon William Randolph Hearst, when it was on the market, telegraphed his

English agent: "WANT BUY ENGLISH CASTLE." His agent put him off: "NOT A BATH IN THE PLACE…SERVANTS QUARTERS DOWN DUNGEONS."

Did Hearst ever buy an English castle? The answer is: No; he bought a Welsh one! This was St. Donat's Castle, acquired in 1925 for £130,000. Hearst had his first sight of it in 1928—all 135 rooms plus the "dungeons." St Donat's was a concentric castle, and its twelfth-century remains, with crenellated curtain walls, towers and gatehouse with portcullis, surrounded by a natural moat of sea and valley, all testified to its

Above: *Bodiam Castle, in East Sussex, England, built between 1385 and 1388, is one of the most picturesque castles of its time. Sited in the middle of an artificial lake, it was designed to defend against French raids and as an extremely comfortable residence for Sir Edward Dalyngrygge, an experienced soldier. The building displays defensive features typical of medieval castles as well as elements of the fortified manor houses that supplanted them in England.*

antiquity. Hearst has been described by his biographer W.A. Swanberg as a man who saw himself as "a Tudor, a Bourbon, a Hapsburg, a prince of absolute power, surrounded by beauty and power." Power he certainly had, and beauty he bought. He supervised every detail of St. Donat's extensive restoration and furnishing, reportedly declaring that "Its beauty overwhelms me….One feels the throb of romance as one walks in the grounds around its wondrous castle walls." St Donat's later became a campus of the Atlantic College, populated with students from all over the world.

We have still another American to thank for the restoration and preservation of a residence rooted in English history: Hever Castle, closely tied to the famous Tudor monarch Henry VIII and his six wives, only one of whom survived him in his ruthless quest for a legitimate son and heir to the throne. William de Hever was responsible for building the original late-medieval fortress with its moat, portcullis and drawbridge, and the family of the ill-fated Anne Boleyn added a Tudor dwelling house within the walls. Some four centuries later, William Waldorf Astor, an American immigrant who would become the first Viscount Astor of Hever Castle, purchased the property. He restored the structure and redecorated the interior, adding some magnificent paneling. In the spirit of American enterprise, he added a village of Tudor-style cottages with interconnecting guest rooms, servants' quarters, kitchens and other offices joined to the castle by a covered bridge across the moat. The gardens were much enlarged and a huge lake added. The castle is now open to the public, and the Tudor village is available for conferences and private parties.

No book on castles would be complete without mention of the famous home of the British royal family, Windsor Castle.

Left: Scotney Castle, in Kent, England, was built around 1380 for the same purpose as its neighbor, Bodiam—to provide protection from raids by the French. Nearby Rye and Winchelsea on the coast had both recently been sacked. The castle was designed as a freestanding residence surrounded by a curtain wall with drum towers at each corner, one of which, now topped by a seventeenth-century conical roof, still survives, as do the original machicolations. The moat and surrounding marshland were achieved by diverting the River Bewl.

Above: Leeds Castle, Kent, has been called "the loveliest castle in the world." Built on the site of the homestead of a ninth-century Saxon king, it is certainly one of the oldest in England. A cousin of William the Conqueror built a Norman castle here, which became the favored residence of many English kings, including Henry VIII, and home to six English queens. Its fabric reflects changing architectural styles over the centuries, and it has been carefully and sympathetically restored by a modern owner.

Like the Tower of London, it originated in William the Conqueror's desire to secure his acquisitions, and both structures have been possessions of the English monarchy ever since. Windsor was a favorite residence of Henry I, and additions and improvements continued long after his reign. The motte was shored up and underpinned to take a stone shell keep, and a second shell constructed within the first was given more effective foundations. Henry II improved the defenses, and the castle received, and survived, its baptism of fire when besieged by King John's enemies in 1216. Great rooms of state appeared during the time of Henry III, or earlier. Edward III remodeled them to create a true palace, housing the largest royal hall in England after Westminster. Windsor was "reinvented" for Charles II, and an engraving shows him holding the Garter Feast in St George's Hall about 1668. George IV (reigned 1820–30) made so many alterations that one needs an architect's trained eye to recognize traces of some of the castle's medieval buildings.

George IV's aim was to produce a modern, medieval-style palace that looked like the romantic image of a castle, and the results are there today for all to see. Towers were provided with corbelled and machicolated parapets, which Edward II would certainly not have recognized. To add insult to injury, the height of the circular keep on the original motte had to be doubled. This was achieved with tremendous ingenuity, since the additional weight would have caused the whole structure to collapse without extensive and skillful architectural work. The original base was "sleeved" with bricks, and the new extension was completely hollow, the ancient motte being underpinned with extremely long steel piles. (In 1987–88 it was discovered that the whole founda-

tion had to be replaced, which was achieved by inserting a concrete ring beam seated on additional piles drilled into the chalk motte—a project ongoing until 1992). However, there was no public outcry at what we could call desecration: on the contrary, this changed landscape was very popular, since it reflected the spirit of the time. All over Europe, ancient castles were being "medievalized" and new buildings created in the Gothic style. Queen Victoria, whose reign saw an excess of quasi-castles, not only in Britain but throughout Europe, and her German husband Albert, were enthusiastic medievalists. They added their own "improvements" to Windsor, and built a magnificent modern edifice in Scotland alongside the ruins of a "proper castle" at

Below: Inspired by Sir Walter Scott's Ivanhoe, *the Norman-style Penrhyn Castle, Gwynedd, Wales, was commissioned in 1827 for a slate millionaire who built on the site of earlier royal castle/residences. The 115-foot (35.1m) keep was modeled on the Norman keep of Rochester Castle (see page 43), while other features, like the machicolations seen on the mural towers, reflect later medieval innovations.*

Above: Despite its European appearance, this castle, nineteenth-century Gothic Revival-style with a hint of Renaissance, is located on an island in the Hudson River, New York. Named for its owner, a businessman of Scottish descent, Bannerman Castle was built between 1900 and 1917 on Pollepel Island for the purpose of housing Frank Bannerman VI's considerable collection of weapons.

Balmoral, in Aberdeenshire. This has a keep/tower/donjon/*Bergfried* complete with its machicolations and crenellations, with brattices on three corners.

Another prime example of this trend is Castell Coch in Wales, overlooking the river near Cardiff. Traces of a medieval castle were probably here when the wealthy Marquess of Bute built himself a brand-new "castle" there in 1872, reportedly based on the plans of a thirteenth-century building. If this is the case, the massive, sharply pointed anti-artillery bastions must be anachronistic. Eastnor Castle (1812–15), in Hertfordshire, is another good English example of an exuberant nineteenth-century Gothic Revival-style fantasy spawned by wealth created during the Industrial Revolution.

Germany, too, provides abundant examples of pseudo-castles, although there the fashion was to restore rather than to rebuild. Between 1900 and 1908, the German kaiser (a title the king of Prussia had assumed in 1871) rebuilt the Hohkönigsburg in what was then German Alsace. His objective was to restore it to its condition in 1480, when its owners were the Grafs Thierstein, but experts found fault with the authenticity of the restoration. In Bavaria, King Ludwig II built the epitome of a mythical Arthurian castle on the ruins of Burg Vorderhohenschwangau. The knights of Schwangau dated back to the twelfth century, and in 1428 Ulrich von Schwangau gave each of his sons one of his four castles: Schwanstein, Frauenstein, and Vorder- and Hinterhohenschwangau. The

From Castle to Castle-mansion

Herstmonceux, East Sussex (main gatefold photograph), was one of the first brick castles in England. The license to build was granted in 1441 to Roger de Fiennes, treasurer to Henry VI. Defensive features of the imposing rectangular structure include tall mural towers, a substantial gatehouse with arrow loops, machicolations and fighting platform, and the wide moat in which the castle itself is set. Effective as a military stronghold, Herstmonceux was one of the forerunners of the castle-mansions that became prevalent during the fifteenth century. As one of its more recent roles, it housed the Royal Observatory between 1948 and 1989.

Prague, the capital city of the Czech Republic, on the River Vltava, was founded in 1310 by King John of Bohemia. The castle (above), the Hradcany, is colocated with St. Vitus's cathedral and still towers over the city. It came to promi-

nence when Charles IV, king of Bohemia and Germany, became the Holy Roman Emperor, using the castle as his palace. The castle also featured in the later Hussite Wars and was the site of the event that triggered the bloody Thirty Years' War (1618), when Protestants threw two officials through a window to land unhurt in a dung heap—an incident that became known as the Defenestration of Prague.

Drummond Castle, Tayside, Scotland (overleaf), is a mansion set in glorious gardens, but the remains of the original fifteenth-century tower-house can still clearly be seen on the left of the picture as the entrance to the later residence. Cromwell's Parliamentarian troops considerably damaged the property in 1650. Now a popular tourist attraction, the castle's most recent claim to fame was to provide the setting for the 1990s film "Rob Roy."

first of these castles was refurbished in 1833 and became Schloss Hohenschwangau, which we can visit today. Vorderhohenschwangau was the site of Ludwig's new castle, known as Schloss Neuschwanstein, begun in 1869. It expressed the king's obsession with the noble, quasi-mythical roots of the German people. Thus Neuschwanstein is a dream— a step toward finding the Holy Grail—and to experience it in its beautiful mountainous setting is an opportunity to share that exalted dream for a while.

Unfortunately, the ancient Wewelsburg, near Paderborn, which had been restored in the seventeenth century, became a symbol of infamy in 1934 when Heinrich Himmler made the stonghold the spiritual headquarters of the S.S.—the "Order" designed to shape and support Nazi ideology, aping (the word is carefully chosen) the Order of the Teutonic Knights. Himmler saw himself as the Grand Master of this order and converted the Wewelsburg, at tremendous expense, into a veritable citadel of oppres-

Opposite: The Château de Chenonceaux, on the River Cher, is one of the most magnificent in the valley of the Loire. The first owners of the site, the Marques family, had to demolish their castle in 1414, having taken arms against their king. However, they soon built another, complete with a mill built on massive pillars set in the river. The castle came into the possession of one of Charles VIII's officials, Thomas Bohier, and he and his wife rebuilt Chenonceaux (1513–19) in its present stunning form, using the substructure of the mill. The famous 200-foot (60m) gallery in the river was commissioned by Catherine de Medici in the mid sixteenth century.

Left: Castell Coch is a fine example of the Victorian desire for all things medieval, including the status of a castle owner. The wealthy third Marquess of Bute employed William Burgess to build this splendid fake in the late nineteenth century. It even has a dungeon.

sion, where the mythology of the "Master Race" was acted out in a bizarre form of ancestor worship directed toward the establishment of the Thousand-year Reich.

In France, a trip down the Loire or the Seine shows that many of the nation's magnificent châteaux-forts have become handsome and impressive châteaux—mansions and palaces with large windows in place of the former arrow and gun loops. Historic Saumur, almost an icon for the lover of things medieval, and well known through the illustrations of the medieval Book of Hours, the *Très Riches Heures du Duc de Berry*, has been split horizontally. Stout bastions remain at the base as traces of its proud military past, and the fairy-tale beauty depicted in so many ancient prints has been

Left and opposite: Schloss Neuschwanstein in Bavaria, Germany, was commissioned by "Mad" King Ludwig II of Bavaria, and work commenced under the supervision of architect Eduard Riedal in 1869. The design was influenced by C. Jank, who created the sets for Wagner's operas, which were based on Germanic myths and romanticized legends of the Middle Ages. If the castle was intended to remind us of those times, and to epitomize Ludwig's vision of a mystical dream castle, it succeeded.

Overleaf: The Grand Château de Chantilly, on the River Nonette, some 25 miles (40 km) northeast of Paris, was built in 1870–82 by Henri, Duc d'Aumale, whose father, Louis Philippe, had inherited it from the Condé family in 1830. It is called the Musée Condé because the first Grand Château was built here in the eighteenth century by Louis the Great Condé, who made it one of the most magnificent in France. This was destroyed during the French Revolution. No trace remains of the earliest castle on this site, which dates from before the tenth century.

Right: The Torre de Belem is an outstanding example of Iberian defensive architecture of the sixteenth century. It stands near the north bank of the River Tagus, designed to protect the port of Lisbon, capital city of Portugal, particularly from its predatory neighbor and rival, Spain. Sea trade, especially with its colonies in South America and the East, was vital to the prosperity of this maritime kingdom. Francesco de Arruda built the fortress in 1515–21: it consists of a massive rectangular tower, richly decorated with crenellations and domed turrets, surrounded by a hexagonal crenellated wall set with embrasures for cannon, and with a bartizan on each of the six angles.

maintained in the comfortable dwelling on top. It is now a museum. Other French strongholds, including Château Gaillard, which withstood a sixteen-month siege before the garrison's water ran out, and Chinon, where Philippe le Bel once imprisoned the Templars, are crumbling ruins. The many religious wars that have shattered France, to say nothing of the destruction wrought by the dynastic wars and the excesses of the French Revolution, have not been kind to French castles. This can be seen in the Dordogne, an area as rich in castles as any in Europe, ravaged by de Montfort and savaged in the Hundred Years War. Many castles there have been well restored and can be visited, but there are all too many "romantic" ruins.

One bittersweet story of a castle's resurrection began in the early 1930s, when Joséphine Baker, the African-American cabaret artist, embraced by the French as "the Charleston Queen of Paris," saw the elegant Château Les Milandes (1488) near Sarlat and fell in love with it. During World War II, Baker was an active member of the French Resistance, for which she was rewarded by General Charles de Gaulle with the Legion of Honour with Rosette. After the war, she bought Les Milandes, refurbished it and found peace and tranquility as well as a new aim in life. As she told Pope Pius XII, she intended to adopt orphaned children from all over the world and give them a happy childhood there, in order to "fight racism and proclaim the unity of the human race." Sadly, the project, which got off to a good start, eventually foundered through lack of funds, but it is a welcome variation on the themes of cruelty and hardship so often associated with castles.

Although their builders may be dead and buried, the castles that have played such a significant role in our history retain their

vitality. They are windows into our past, providing as many lessons and examples of both good and bad as their contemporaries, the Gothic cathedrals. It is encouraging to see so many European schoolchildren taking field trips to castles in their localities. And the popularity of castles with foreign visitors accompanied by many excellent guides must foster the growing awareness of the "unity of the human race," as peo-

ple from around the world realize that their own histories share the evolutionary throes exemplified in these architectural landmarks. It is also gratifying to see that many of the wonderful castles of Spain and Portugal, where two cultures clashed and merged, are being made more accessible through the *Paradores* and the *Pousades*, plans whereby visitors may stay in converted castles and imbibe their histories along with regional cuisines and drinks. General Sir John Hackett, a renowed warrior and academic, wrote in his foreword to the excellent book *Castles, A History and Guide* (Blandford Press, 1980): "Castles, thrusting out from the landscape in an essentially assertive way, are bold and splendid things. They are as significant in the political, social and economic aspects of our history as they are beautiful to look at." That says it all.

The Principles of War

Castles were essentially a military solution to problems that might well have had their origins in economic, political, historic, or religious roots. They were therefore unlikely to provide a complete and lasting answer to all or many of the complex causes of strife throughout the Middle Ages. When the purpose of the castle builder was mainly defensive, the chances of success were greater than when there were several different functions, sometimes conflicting, intended for one castle. The reader might find a brief glimpse of the principles of war helpful background to the science and skills of castle building and siege warfare during the Middle Ages, or, indeed, to the history of fortresses since humans started building and attacking them. We shall be looking at the British Army's principles, mainly because they are simple and well established. Most modern armies have their own similar versions. Principles, like conflict, are timeless. Although cultures, methods and technology may change, human nature does not.

SELECTION AND MAINTENANCE OF THE AIM

British officer cadets are taught that in military decision-making, selection of the aim should have more time allotted to it than the rest of the process put together. Before selecting his aim, the wise castle builder had to make sure that he had all the relevant facts at his fingertips, including the aim of his military superior; had reviewed all the desired purposes for his castle; selected the most important or pressing requirements; and prioritized the remainder. A good commander would have made certain that all his subordinates were informed of his aim and, ideally, the reasons for its selection, so that they could act in the spirit of the operation. Having selected the aim, the commander could then work out his plan to maintain it, bearing the remaining principles in mind. If the correct selection was made in the first place, there should be no reason to be diverted from achieving it, unless—crucially—the original circumstances changed significantly. It would then become imperative to select a new aim, alter priorities, or ask for advice from the superior. Many calamitous military defeats were brought about by an obstinate or ill-advised determination to stick to an aim that had become hopelessly unachievable.

MAINTENANCE OF MORALE

This is a prerequisite of success for any military force, and a good commander would ignore it at his peril. There is no simple rule to achieve this, but high morale can enable success in the face of very great odds, while an attempt to destroy the enemy's morale can help to bring about his collapse. Religion, patriotism, fellowship, welfare, greed, hate, fear, hunger and disease are just a few of the many factors that affect morale.

OFFENSIVE ACTION

This apparently obvious maxim is surprisingly often forgotten. A besieger might have been content to sit out a siege, waiting for hunger to force the defenders to surrender. A castellan might have been tempted to keep his head down behind the parapet until relief appeared. Both would have been wrong. There are many examples of defenders sallying out and defeating the surrounding enemy. A besieged garrison should constantly attack the enemy with every possible means, and the experienced besieger should, similarly, keep up an active attack, with every available resource, to wear down the defenders and sap their resources of men, material and morale. Both sides should seek to inflict maximum casualties.

SURPRISE

Very often, success has been achieved by surprising an enemy. The sudden sally of the defenders has been mentioned, but just as important would be the concealed approach and sudden attack before an effective defense could be prepared. A castle designer and defender would take great pains to anticipate and plan responses to surprise attack.

ECONOMY OF EFFORT

This principle was once combined with concentration, its corollary. Essentially, it warns against wasting effort instead of concentrating it when required. It was sometimes necessary to take calculated risks when allocating resources in order to maintain a mobile reserve, for example. The requirement for security could, mistakenly, lead a commander to spread his forces thinly around a perimeter, positioning them in places where they could not suddenly be included in a concentration.

CONCENTRATION OF FORCE

This would be of the greatest importance in castle design. Success is often achieved by bringing the maximum numbers together rapidly at a strategic time and place to achieve military superiority. Defenders needed to be able to rush on wide wall-walks to the specific point in the defenses where the attacker had concentrated his forces, and not be hindered on the curtain walls by mural towers with barred gates. The German Army based much of their tactical doctrine on defining and building a *Schwerpunkt* (point of main emphasis), as they called it, and history tells us how successful this could be: the British and French were surprised in 1940, for example, by the concentration of German armor in the Ardennes.

SECURITY

Physical security was uppermost in every castle builder's mind, and we have seen how important this was in our study of the evolution of fortification, ending with moats and drawbridges, the massive gatehouses, the *Schildmauer* and the artillery fortress. Caesar knew its value when he built defenses against attack from a relieving army around forces besieging a Celtic fort. Security also entailed keeping one's strengths, weaknesses, dispositions and plans secret from an enemy, and taking precautions against spies and treachery. A poisoned well or sudden outbreak of disease could bring about a castle's downfall more effectively than an attempt to batter a breach in the walls.

FLEXIBILITY

It was probably Clausewitz who first said that no plan lasts longer than the first encounter with the enemy (although this is often attributed to General Field Marshal von Moltke), and it was the wise commander who, having first sought to predict and counter every possible move of the enemy, still had the ability and resources to react swiftly to the unexpected. It is a bad plan that cannot be modified, whether by attacker or defender, and an experienced commander would have exercised his troops for swift redeployment to counter sudden and unexpected moves of the enemy. Flexibility requires mental agility under stress, and is the hallmark of a successful soldier.

COOPERATION

The experienced commander of ancient times knew the value of "team spirit," even though the term had not yet been invented. He would also have understood the need for the many skilled craftsmen and experts to be coordinated (knights, sappers, miners, engineers, archers, men-at-arms and fireworkers, to name but a few) and to be applied at the right place and time. Many circumstances required the cooperation of reluctant allies, who could easily turn hostile or desert. Indeed, forces were frequently composed of men who owed allegiance to the same lord, yet often had no common language or even any great trust in each other. Another modern term for a long-understood military principle is "synergy," which applies when several people or forces working together have the potential to produce an effect greater than the sum of their potential individual effects.

ADMINISTRATION

Shortly after World War II, cadets were told that Field Marshal Montgomery had added this principle to the list, following administrative bungles including one in which the cargo of the first ship to be unloaded upon the invasion of Italy consisted largely of garbage cans rather than ammunition. It seems so obvious that an army must be clothed, fed, watered and supplied with adequate weapons, arms and ammunition and, indeed, everything else necessary to enable it to achieve its commanders aim. Nevertheless, many military failures have been brought about because administrative requirements were neglected. The castle facing a siege had to maintain sufficient stocks of everything that might be needed, and the castellan would know exactly how long they would last. Getting this sum wrong could end in disaster. Until recently most armies depended on the resources of the country they were invading or passing through, but there was a big difference between paying for supplies and stealing them. The besieger was required to send foraging parties progressively farther afield to keep his force supplied, usually by robbing elusive peasants. If he could afford to pay, however, peasants would willingly bring food to him for profit. The Crusaders learned (the hard way) the lesson of good administration in a barren land, and their systems for acquiring and storing water, for example, were astonishingly sophisticated for the times. A large baggage train could cause a tremendous delay and be vulnerable to attack, but it could make the difference between success and failure. Edward I demonstrated his grasp of administration when he built his Welsh castles to be supplied by sea, and it interesting to know that Wellington honed his administrative skills in the deserts of India.

GLOSSARY

*Words in **boldface** refer to separate entries.*

Allure: another name for **wall-walk**.

Arrow slit: *see* **loop**.

Ashlar: cut or squared stone for building and facing.

Bailey: walled enclosure or courtyard.

Barbican: outer defensive work, especially in front of a gate.

Bastion: a low solid projection from a wall or tower, often sharply angled, to provide extra protection.

Battlements: *see* **crenellations**.

Barmkin: enclosure around a **peel** (or **pele**) tower.

Bartizan (above): projecting tower or **turret** supported on **corbels**, especially at a corner.

Batter: inclined or splayed base of a wall (**talus**).

Bawn: a walled enclosure.

Belfry (right): siege tower (from Old French *berfrei*).

Bergfried: a tall, narrow tower in German-speaking countries (many alternative spellings in Old German).

Berm: level area between **moat** and base of **curtain wall**.

Bombard: an early form of cannon.

Brattice: *see* **hoarding**.

Broch: Scottish tower, circular in plan, usually with two concentric shells.

Buttress: projection from a wall for additional support.

Castellan: person in charge of a castle.

Castle-guard: period of service (duty) in a castle for a feudal knight.

Cat: roofed protective shed for sappers and miners at base of a wall.

Chemise: a wall surrounding a **keep** or joining onto it.

Chemin de ronde: *see* **wall-walk**.

Concentric castle: one surrounded by two or more concentric (**curtain**) walls, the outer ones lower than the inner, to allow two levels of archers to fire on the same target.

Constable: senior official in charge of a castle in the owner's absence.

Corbel: load-bearing masonry projection from a wall.

Crenel (above): space between two **merlons** on a **parapet** *see also* **crenellations**.

Crenellations: **parapet** with alternating **merlons** and **crenels**, castellated.

Curtain wall: wall enclosing a castle, or connecting two towers or **bastions**.

Dead ground: an area out of sight of the enemy, thus providing protection.

Ditch: a wide trench to hinder the enemy, normally dry.

Donjon: Norman French for what is called a **keep** or great-tower; not a prison.

Drawbridge: one that can be drawn up or swiveled to prevent an enemy crossing. Normally over a **moat** and at least one in a gateway and **barbican**.

Drum-tower: large, circular tower, usually low and squat.

En bec (adj.): beaked; describing a tower pointing toward an attacker's likely approach.

Enceinte: the fortified perimeter of a castle; the main enclosure.

Embrasure (left): small opening in a fortified **parapet**, usually splayed on the inside, for an archer or cannon.

Flanking: the means of directing fire along the length of a wall, normally from projecting towers or **bartizans**.

Forebuilding: a strong constructed extension on the side of a **keep** to cover the door, usually containing a **portcullis** and **drawbridge**, and entered by an unprotected stairway or ramp.

Ganerbenburg: A term denoting a castle in German-speaking lands shared by several branches of the same family.

Garderobe: latrine.

Gatehouse: a stout building designed to strengthen the castle's main entrance, often the residence of the **castellan** or **constable**.

Great hall: the main residence and accommodation of the lord, when not located in the **keep**.

Glacis: smooth stone incline used as a defense.

Gun loop: *see* **loop**.

Hoarding (right): temporary timber gallery projecting from a tower or wall-head to provide vertical defense, also called a **brattice**.

Hornwork: outwork.

Keep: relatively modern English word for donjon or great tower: in earlier times, the major defensive structure and residence of the lord, and the last refuge.

Lists: tiltyard for jousting, normally outside the castle walls.

Loop (left): narrow aperture from which to fire arrows or guns; hence arrow loop, gun loop.

Machicolation: projecting stone gallery on a tower or wall-head, enabling an enemy at the base to be attacked from above.

Mangonel: siege engine.

Merlon: the upwardly projecting part of a **battlemented parapet**.

Meutrières: *see* **murder-holes**.

Moat: a water-filled ditch surrounding a castle, often formed partially by diverting a river.

Motte: a small hill, usually artificial, on the summit of which a castle was built, originally of timber (motte-and-bailey castle).

Mural: in or on a wall; as in "mural tower."

Murder-holes: holes in the roof of a passageway through which an enemy could be attacked from above.

Oubliette: French name given for a dungeon below ground level wherein a prisoner could be forgotten.

Palisade: timber fence or defensive screen.

Parapet: low wall on top of and outside the main wall.

Pele (or **peel**): tower-house or **keep**-like building; a term used especially on the Scottish border.

Pilaster: a flat **buttress** projecting slightly from a wall.

Portcullis (above): a heavy iron-tipped grille that could be lowered quickly to block an entrance. Some **gatehouses** or **forebuildings** had more than one.

Postern: a lesser and privy (private) gateway.

Rampart: a mound of earth or stone raised as a defense for a castle or town.

Ravelin: outwork with two faces at salient angles to each other.

Revetment: a retaining wall or facing.

Ringwork: any earthen defensive enclosure.

Scarp: slope on inner side of **ditch**.

Schildmauer (shield-wall): in German-speaking lands, a term used to describe an especially strong or high wall built to provide extra protection to a vulnerable approach.

Shell keep: circular or oval wall surrounding interior portion of a castle, often around the summit of a **motte**.

Spur: solid angular projection built at the base of a tower or wall to prevent mining and divert projectiles.

Slight (verb): to render a castle indefensible by partially destroying.

Talus: *see* **batter**.

Trebuchet (left): extremely powerful siege engine worked by counterpoise to project large missiles.

Turret: a slender tower projecting from the roof of a larger tower.

Wall-walk (below): pathway on the **ramparts** behind the **crenellations**.

Ward: *see* **bailey**.

Yett: strong iron gate, usually in the form of a grid.

INDEX

BIBLIOGRAPHY

Anderson, William. *Castles of Europe.* Omega Books Ltd, 1984.
Asley, Maurice. *William I.* Book Club Associates, 1973.
Barton, Stuart. *Castles in Britain.* Lyle Publications, 1973.
Bridge, Antony. *The Crusades.* Granada, 1980.
Brown, Allen R., Consultant. *Castles: A History and Guide.* Blandford Press, 1980.
———. *Castles from the Air.* Cambridge University Press, 1989.
———. *English Castles.* B.T.Batsford Ltd, 1954/1976.
———. *The Normans.* Boydell Press, 1984.
Corfis and Wolfe, Eds. *The Medieval City Under Siege.* The Boydell Press, 1999.
Coss, Peter. *The Knight in Medieval England 1000–1400.* Alan Sutton Publishing Ltd, 1993.
Davis, R.H.C. *The Normans And Their Myths.* Thames and Hudson, 1997.
Forde-Johnston. *Castles and Fortifications of Britain and Ireland.* J Publications, 1973.
Foss, Michael. *Chivalry.* Book Club Associates, 1975.
Fry, Plantagenet Somerset. *Castles of Britain and Ireland.* David and Charles, 1996.
Fryer, Jonathan. *The Great Wall of China.* Book Club Associates, 1975.
Gascoigne, Christina. *Castles of Britain.* Thames and Hudson, 1975.
Goodwin, Jason. *Lords of the Horizons: A History of the Ottoman Empire.* Chatto and Windus, 1998.
Gravett, Christopher. *Castle.* Dorling Kindersley, 1994.
Grimble, Ian. *Castles of Scotland.* BBC Books, 1987.
Hallam, Elizabeth. Ed. *Chronicle of the Crusades.* Bramley Books, 1996.
Hansmann, Wilfred. *Schlösser der Loire.* Dumont, 1997.
Harpur, James. *Inside the Medieval World.* Cassel, 1995.
Hay, Denys. *Europe in the Fourteenth and Fifteenth Centuries.* Longman, 1996
Hindley, Geoffrey. *Medieval Warfare.* Wayland Publishers, 1971.
Humble, Richard. *English Castles.* Artus Books, Orion Publishing Group, 1984.
Johnson, Paul. *The National Trust Book of British Castles.* Weidenfeld and Nicholson, 1978.
Keegan, John. *A History of Warfare.* Pimlico, 1994.
Kennedy, Hugh. *Crusader Castles.* Cambridge University Press, 1994.
Kern, Paul Bentley. *Ancient Siege Warfare.* Souvenir Press Ltd, 1999.
Kightly, Charles. *Strongholds of the Realm.* Thames and Hudson, 1979.
Koch, H.W. *Medieval Warfare.* Bison Books Ltd, 1978.
Kordel, Matthias. *Die Schönsten Schlösser und Burgen in der Eifel.* Wartburg Verlag, 1999.
Libal, Doproslav. *Castles of Britain and Europe.* Bookmart Ltd, 1999.
Macaulay, David. *City, Castle, Cathedral.* William Collins Sons & Co Ltd, 1979.
Macqueen, J.G. *The Hittites and their Contemporaries In Asia Minor.* Thames and Hudson, 1975.
Morris, J.E. *The Welsh Wars Of Edward I.* Sutton Publishing, 1998.
Mountfield, David. *Castles and Castle Towns of Great Britain.* Bracken Books, 1995.
Newark, Timothy. *Medieval Warfare.* Jupiter Books, 1975.
Newbolt, Henry. *Stories from Froissart.* Wells, Gardner, Warton & Co, 1900.
Peters, Ellis. *Strongholds and Sanctuaries: Borderland of England and Wales.* Alan Sutton Publishing Ltd, 1993.
Pevsner, Nikolaus. *An Outline of European Architecture.* Penguin Books Ltd, 1943.
Piper, Otto. *Burgenkunde.* Weltbild Verlag, 1912, 1994.
Poux, Joseph. *The City of Carcassonne.* Toulouse.-Impr. et Libr. Édouard Privat, 1922.
Reader's Digest, Eds. *Album Des Châteaux De France.* Sélection du Reader's Digest, 1975.
Simpson, Douglas W. *Castles from the Air.* Country Life Ltd, 1949.
Smithers, David Walden. *Castles in Kent.* John Halliwell Publications, 1980.
Somerville, Donald. *Castles.* Bison Books Ltd, 1995.
Tejada, Luis Monreal. *Medieval Castles Of Spain.* Könemann, 1999.
Toy, Sidney. *Castles* (First Edition). William Heinemann Ltd, 1939.
Toy, Sidney. *The Castles of Great Britain.* Heinemann, 1966.
Turnbull, Stephen. *The Book of the Medieval Knight.* Cassel, 1985.
Warner, Philip. *The Medieval Castle.* Book Club Associates, 1973.